KW-483-247

The Employment of People with Disabilities in Small and Medium-sized Enterprises

EUROPEAN FOUNDATION

for the Improvement of Living and Working Conditions

Wyattville Road, Loughlinstown, Co. Dublin, Ireland
Tel: +353 1 204 3100 Fax: +353 1 282 6456/282 4209
E-mail: postmaster@eurofound.ie.

Cataloguing data can be found at the end of this publication

Luxembourg: Office for Official Publications of the European Communities, 1998

ISBN 92-828-2949-9

Printed in Ireland

The Employment of People with Disabilities in Small and Medium-sized Enterprises

Nexus Research Co-operative

The European Foundation for the Improvement of Living and Working Conditions is an autonomous body of the European Union, created to assist the formulation of future policy on social and work-related matters.

This report has been written for the Foundation by Morgan Carpenter of Nexus Research Co-operative, Dublin.

Foreword

According to Eurostat estimates, 12% of the European Union population suffers from a disability: proportionately, their employment rate is substantially lower and their unemployment rate higher than for others in the labour force.

Small and medium sized enterprises (SMEs) have a large potential for job creation. We ask, how people with disabilities could have better access to employment in such companies? In this report, the question is addressed by focusing on the opinions of people with disabilities and their employers, managers and co-workers.

The results are based on company case-studies from six Member States: France, Germany, Ireland, Netherlands, Spain and United Kingdom. In spite of the differences in their legal frameworks, employment practices and culture, the similarities among these countries seem to be many. In addition, it is encouraging to note the practicability of the approaches found to resolve the problems, which have brought benefit not only to those with disabilities, but also to their companies and to society as a whole.

We are grateful to the authors of this report for their effort and patience in summarising the cases. We are grateful, too, to the researchers who prepared the case studies, the members of the Administrative Board and the Committee of Experts of the Foundation who reviewed them and the members of the coordination and evaluation committees of the research project.

The project benefited also from the active collaboration of the services of the European Commission (DGV). In the Foundation, it was implemented under the responsibility of Jaume Costa and Isy Vromans, Research Managers.

We hope that this report will give food for thought to people with disabilities, to policymakers and to the social partners on how the access of people with disabilities to employment in SMEs can be improved.

Clive Purkiss

Director

Eric Verborgh

Deputy Director

Contents

Chapter 1   Introduction

People with disabilities are recognised to be one of the most disadvantaged sections of society. They face considerable barriers in accessing the labour market, education and training opportunities and social facilities. These are a product not only of actual impairments that limit the actions people with disabilities are able to perform, but also of attitudes and an environment that does not take account of their needs.

Each EU Member State has adopted a range of measures to promote the integration and employment of people with disabilities. There is an existing body of comparative research on the legislative framework for these measures, and on employment patterns in enterprises in particular Member States. Two significant gaps arise in the material available.

Despite constituting a major proportion of the business sector, there is little data on the role and experience of small and medium sized enterprises (SMEs) in the employment of people with disabilities. SMEs, those that employ less than 500 employees, provide more than two thirds of EU employment and are regarded as the greatest potential job creators. However, their small size and large number has excluded them from study: not only are they more difficult to identify, access and research, they might also be exempt from many statutory obligations including what, in many EU Member States, is the most visible employment promotion measure: a statutory quota for the employment of people with disabilities.

There is also little information currently available on the practical effects and impact of different policies on employers. Existing study, where it has considered the effect of public measures, has focused on the recruitment of people with disabilities, particularly those that are recruited under specific programmes or schemes, and particularly those that have been recruited by larger, easily identifiable enterprises. Little is currently known about decision making processes outside the framework of formal programmes, and little is known about the retention and development of employees with disabilities.

The aim of this study is to determine how and why small and medium sized enterprises recruit and employ people with disabilities. It considers the processes by which an employer identifies a need to employ someone, a person with a disability seeks employment, and a contractual relationship is established and maintained.

Studies have been conducted in six Member States, commissioned by the European Foundation for the Improvement of Living and Working Conditions or national governments. The emphasis of the studies was qualitative, focusing on the perceptions and experience of employers and their employees, and a case study approach was adopted. Each of the six national studies has been published as a Working Paper by the Foundation.

This report is concerned with the outcomes of these six studies and the lessons that can be drawn by considering issues and consequences that are both common to all or unique to some Member States. Following an explanation of the general methodological approach adopted, the regulatory framework in each of the studied countries is presented. This chapter seeks to summarise the policy context rather than present a detailed analysis which is available elsewhere. The twenty-two cases are then summarised followed by a detailed analysis of their implications. Conclusions and recommendations complete the report.

The language used to describe different forms of disability in each national report varies according to local usage and the preferences and understandings of the report translators. While considered appropriate in their original language, some terms used in translation might be felt to carry negative associations or connotations. To ensure greater clarity, readability and avoid the use of terms no longer considered appropriate, the language used here has been standardised, except where quoted directly from national reports.

The National Researchers

The national reports were written by the following teams:

France — Dominique Velche, Centre Technique National D'Etudes et de Recherches sur les Handicaps et les Inadaptations (CTNERHI), Paris.

Germany — Arno Georg and Martina Stackelbeck, assisted by Silke Kutz, Sozialforschungsstelle (sfs) Dortmund.

Ireland — Brian Dillon and Finola Ó Siochrú, Nexus Research Co-operative, Dublin.

Netherlands — Edwin de Vos, Work and Health Division, NIA TNO, Amsterdam.

Spain — Carlos Pereda, Miguel Angel de Prada and Walter Actis, IOÉ Collective, Madrid.

United Kingdom — Anne Corden and Patricia Thornton, Social Policy Research Unit (SPRU), University of York.

This Consolidated Report was written by Morgan Carpenter of Nexus Research Co-operative, Dublin.

The project was managed by Jaume Costa of the European Foundation for the Improvement of Living and Conditions, Dublin.

Chapter 2   Methodology

Introduction

The emphasis of this study is qualitative, focusing on the perceptions and experience of employers and their employees. Rather than add to the existing body of research on the legislative framework for the promotion of employment of people with disabilities in each Member State, or consider employment patterns in enterprises in selected EU Member States, this study seeks to answer two questions about small and medium sized enterprises ('SMEs'):

- why do (or do not) employers in small and medium sized enterprises employ people with disabilities?

- how do employers in small and medium sized enterprises employ people with disabilities?

A case study approach was adopted to examine these issues, providing ideas and identifying issues which promote or hinder the access of people with disabilities to employment in small and medium sized enterprises.

Six EU Member States participated in the study: France, Germany, Ireland, the Netherlands, Spain and the United Kingdom. In each of these Member States, a local research team produced a national report based on three or more case studies. More information on the methodology followed by each individual research team is presented, together with case study analyses and conclusions, in national reports which have been published as Working Papers by the European Foundation for the Improvement of Living and Working Conditions.

Definition of Disability

As an operational definition the main HELIOS definition was proposed for the purposes of this study:

"disabled people means people with serious impairments, disabilities or handicaps resulting from physical (including sensorial) or mental impairments (including psychological) and restricting or making impossible the performance of an activity or function considered normal for a human being."

The target group in the project therefore included all employees who might be hampered in work performance; encompassing chronically ill people as well as people with more stable disorders.

Given the diversity of criteria used at national level, and also by different bodies within a Member State, the HELIOS definition was not used as the only possible definition. In practical terms, national teams had to be cogniscent of the concepts used, and different groups included in definitions used by institutions in each country.

Case Study Methodology

National research teams were given the opportunity to conduct the case-study research in accordance with their own views and experience, following their own approach and methodologies, the aim being to take into account the particular context of the country and each enterprise. They were also, in some cases, able to re-examine enterprises already known to them.

Within this broad range of possible methodological approaches, guidelines were produced governing the criteria for the cases, required information, possible areas of questioning and an outline of the country report. A checklist of possible relevant factors, instead of very specific questions, was also given, as follows:

Case Study Selection

In some Member States, a single local labour market was selected. In others, case studies were selected from a broader geographical area. Both approaches aimed to allow for the examination of differences due to employee, enterprise and employer characteristics.

The difficulty in constructing a 'representative sample' of enterprises was acknowledged from the outset. However, the selection processes used in each country aimed to allow for useful comparisons to be made between different kinds of enterprise, for example, companies of varying sizes, in different sectors, employing people with different disabilities.

Characteristics of the Enterprise	Characteristics of the Work

Characteristics of the Enterprise

- Sector
- Type of service provided
- Number employed
- Financial/economic position; competition
- Region

Characteristics of the Employee

- Gender, nationality, age
- Education/training
- Employment history
- Disability, limitations
- Medical history
- Work handicap

Recruitment

- Description of the recruitment process
- Factors which played a part in the recruitment
- Why and how
- Company policy on employing people with a disability
- Social policy
- Flexibility of working hours
- Issues at management level
- Colleagues

Characteristics of the Work

- Length of employment
- Job
- Workplace
- Department
- Working hours

Work Adaptations and Accommodations

INTANGIBLE

- Adaptation of working hours
- Adaptation of job
- Rest breaks, evening and weekend duty
- Part-time/alternating duty
- Working hours/hours worked

TANGIBLE

- Adaptation of the workplace
- Transport to and from work

SUPPORT/GUIDANCE

- Positive factors emerging after recruitment
- Negative factors emerging after recruitment

The limited number of case studies meant that it was not easily possible to test some hypotheses at a national level, such as trade sector differences and attitudes towards a range of different disabilities. Consolidating the national reports has enabled some of these issues to be revealed in more detail. The extent of study of cases in which the integration had failed was also limited. Where possible, this was achieved by considering past and other present employees in enterprises studied.

Four different methods were used to identify potential case studies:

- direct contact with employees known to be working in small and medium sized enterprises ('SMEs');

- direct contact with SME employers known to employ people with disabilities;

- developing contacts through the use of intermediaries known to both SME employers and employees with disabilities;

- returning to case study enterprises from a previous study or survey.

In the majority of national studies, the third approach was adopted from the outset. In the British study, the first two methods were fully investigated before adopting the third. As a result, the case study material generated in Britain varied substantially from the three or four complete case studies in other study countries: one full case study; in-depth interviews with two employers who had experience of disabled employees in which 'modelling' techniques were used to explore some of the key issues; and three sets of interviews with disabled employees and the advisers who had helped them secure their jobs.

Direct Contact with Employees

Self-advocacy and other organisations representing the interests of people with disabilities, while aware of larger firms with the reputation of being equal opportunity employers, were frequently unable to suggest enterprises which satisfied the scope of this study, eliminating the possibility of an approach to an employee directly.

In the British study, a number of attempts to identify individual employees were made. The general finding was that issues of confidentiality were paramount, and there were also time and resource constraints for agencies used to identify employees. The researchers were advised by government agencies that help place people in work that they rarely maintain contact, and therefore do not have information about the current circumstances of the people they have placed in work. The Trades Union Congress official for the local labour market studied in Britain was keen to co-operate with the research but was prohibited by a lack of Trades Union contacts due to low levels of unionisation in small businesses. A further attempt at direct recruitment of employees with disabilities was made through an advertisement placed in a local weekly newspaper which was delivered free to 157,000 households in the study area. There were no responses to the advertisement.

In the British study, these case study recruitment problems were thought to arise from a number of reasons including:

- low numbers of people with disabilities who work in small/medium sized private enterprises;

- concentration of people with disabilities in certain forms of employment;

- reluctance among people who do have such employment to identify themselves as disabled, a negative identification which stresses inabilities;

- reluctance of employees to identify their disability to employers, to avoid anticipated stigmatisation or discrimination;

- time and resource constraints among employers;

- reluctance among employers to discuss their recruitment and employment practices;

- low membership of support groups among people with disabilities who work in private businesses, thus limiting ways of accessing people;

- the importance attached to confidentiality among supporting agencies;

- time and resource constraints among supporting agencies;

- possible 'gate-keeping' roles among officials of voluntary and support groups.

Direct Contact with Employers

An alternative approach was to identify a person with a disability employed in an SME and seek their agreement to approach their employer. This was not considered appropriate in the study as it was felt that there could be negative implications for an employee in such a situation.

It was possible to approach employers in enterprises which met enterprise-related study selection criteria. There were problems, however, in the British study in recruiting appropriate employees from among their workforces. The researchers consulted professionals, disability support groups, people with disabilities and academic researchers and found there was general agreement that it was ethically inappropriate for employers to identify or approach individual employees on the basis of their disability status. The approach considered correct was for participating employers to issue an invitation to all employees, to which people who identified themselves as having a disability might respond directly to the researcher if they chose. In practical terms, it was found to be difficult to promote the full distribution of individual invitations to large workforces by employers. There was also the possibility that appropriate employees would not choose to identify themselves or wish to take part. This may be especially likely among people who are keen that their employers do not know about their personal circumstances. The British team's attempts to reach disabled employees of employers who both met selection criteria and had agreed to take part were unsuccessful. Given the resource constraints, it was decided not to pursue this option.

Developing Contacts through Mediators

Each research team was aware of the limitations of confining the choice of company to those who had employed a person with a disability through an agency as opposed to on the open market. Such methods were used largely as a consequence of the elimination of alternative methods of accessing people with disabilities.

The choice of case studies by each national team reflected a desire to test as many different scenarios as possible, including employees with diverse disabilities, small and large businesses, and ones in different trade sectors. These choices reflect difficulties in meeting preferred criteria, the disclosure arrangements preferred by mediators, and also the accuracy of information available on each enterprise and employee prior to interview.

Returning to Case Study Enterprises from a Previous Study

In the German study, nineteen possible case studies were selected from those interviewed as part of a study to evaluate the "Aktion Integration" programme (Richter/Stackelbeck, 1995), which analysed the effect of a labour market programme on the occupational integration of people with severe disabilities to determine the number of permanent employment contracts concluded as a result of the programme. The factors evaluated were:

- the structure of the programme and the conditions for receiving assistance;

- employers' motivation and attitudes towards employing people with disabilities;

- co-operation between the employment authorities' placement service for people with disabilities and the institutions offering support and guidance on employment-related matters (central or local welfare offices).

As a result of the study parameters, all the enterprises were also sourced through mediating organisations, state welfare offices and employment offices. The survey covered four main issues:

- factors which influenced recruitment;

- application and approval procedures;

- the integration of employees with disabilities in the company;

- employment prospects in the company for other employees with disabilities.

As the German interviews were intended to provide information on the practical working and employment conditions of employees in assisted jobs and on the action and motivation of the people involved in the firms, the selection of three cases from the nineteen possible was tailored to cover the widest possible range of distinguishing features, thus enabling structural factors to be identified. Account was also taken of the size of the enterprises, their legal structures and the economic sectors and types of disability involved.

Case Study Implementation

The case studies were carried out in late 1996 and in early 1997, varying from country to country. In each national study, research teams followed a line of questioning that would:

1. Establish the general operational background to the firm;

2. Obtain details on the firm's current policy and procedures in relation to employing people with disabilities;

3. Construct a profile of how the policy and procedures have worked in practice (in relation both to current and past employees);

4. Find out about barriers (from the point of view of employer and employee) to successful recruitment and employment practice;

5. Obtain feedback from respondents on what changes may be needed.

In cases where enterprises employed a person with a particular disability, researchers enquired about possible barriers to employing people with other disabilities.

Wherever possible, three stakeholder representatives were interviewed in each case study: a person representing the employer, the person with a disability, and a third stakeholder in the recruitment or staff development process.

The third stakeholder varied between countries and individual case studies, owning to variations in the sourcing of each case, the varying role of job placement and support agencies, and the relative absence of employee representatives (through Trades Unions or Works Councils) in the SME sector.

Most interviews were carried out face-to-face either at the home or the workplace of the respondent. Where this was not possible, interviews were conducted by telephone.

Case Study Validation

Each national research team engaged in other forms of quantitative or qualitative research to give some more concrete basis to the conclusions reached in the case studies:

- in France, researchers consulted with EPSR (Redeployment Preparation and Monitoring Team) members, officials responsible for the co-ordination of plans for Départements in the Paris region for the integration of people with disabilities;

- in Germany, the research study was closely related to a broader 'Aktion Integration' programme evaluation across 8 employment office districts in North Rhine-Westphalia;

- in Ireland, interviews were conducted with people in organisations representing key 'stakeholder' interests in the provision of services, development of policy and promotion of equality. These included a member of the Commission on Status of People with a Disability (also a Disability Consultant); a representative of Schizophrenia Ireland (a voluntary organisation) involved in 'Worklink', the body's placement service); an Area Manager with the state National Rehabilitation Board, personally involved in the placement of people with different disabilities; and a member of the National Forum of People with Disabilities;

- in the Netherlands, reference was also made to a quantitative survey conducted on behalf of the Dutch Ministry. The 'ZARA' study of 3,300 businesses examined the issues of absenteeism, incapacity for work, working conditions and the reintegration of people with disabilities;

- in Spain, reference was made to a 1992 Municipal Institute for the Disabled study of the 'Attitudes of Private Enterprise towards the Employment of People with Disabilities'. In total, 734 enterprises employing more than 50 people were studied;

- in the United Kingdom, further interviews were conducted with two employers using 'modelling' techniques to establish attitudes to a broad range of situations. Each model case consisted of a photograph of a hypothetical potential employee, and a short account of their skills and qualification, previous work experience and the circumstances of their disability or illness which might affect their work. The employers were invited to give their reactions to what they were shown, and to discuss the issues they would consider if that person applied for a job. The model cases were constructed individually for each employer, to match the occupations and tasks involved in each enterprise. The technique offered advantages in that, since the potential employees were not real, there were no problems in breaching confidentiality, which proved important in the UK study. Two further interviews were conducted with different employers who met the selection criteria. One extended an invitation to her employees, but without response.

Chapter 3

The Context at Member State Level

Introduction

Statistical information on the prevalence of disability has recently become available at a European level, although its accuracy is limited by national differences in methodological approaches, public attitudes, demographic structures, historical experience and general economic conditions.

Methodological differences arise, for example, through different methods of defining disability: based on a medical condition, a social definition of a society that is unable to adapt itself; severity; or registration under specific national policies or programmes.

Perception of what constitutes a disability varies according to individual attitudes and expectations of normality; the financial importance of accessing state support programmes; and, in particular, the influence of prejudice and discrimination. As a result of such disadvantage, disability is rarely seen as a positive form of self-identification.

Demographic differences, such as the age composition of a population, also have a significant bearing: rates of disability increase with age.

Despite these limitations, Eurostat, in 'Disabled Persons, Statistical Data, Second Edition' (1995) presents some general conclusions about the (then 12) Member States:

- approximately 12% of the total population experienced a disability;

- 6-8% of people aged under 60 were considered to experience a disability;

- 4-5% of people aged under 60 were in receipt of disability-related payments;

- "analysis of the percentage of disabled persons by age group revealed a stable and uniform relationship in the Member States" (Eurostat);

- physical (particularly motor) disabilities account for some 50 to 80% of disabilities, sensory impairments for 10 to 18%, and mental disabilities and illnesses for 5 to 15%.

Means of promoting the participation of people with disabilities in the labour market also vary between Member States. Legislation promoting the employment of people with disabilities in European Union Member States has been characterised by Lunt and Thornton (in Employment Policies for Disabled People, Employment Department, UK, 1993), among others, as tending towards compulsory employment measures while countries such as Canada, Australia and the United States have focused more on anti-discrimination and equal opportunities legislation.

A recent review of this publication (Thornton and Lunt, 'Employment Policies for Disabled People in Eighteen Countries: A Review', 1997). suggests that a considerable blurring of these boundaries has occurred. A line can still, however, be drawn to distinguish between countries positioning legislation on disability within the context of a broad anti-discriminatory policy and those operating compartmentalised measures such as quota legislation. While EU countries still tend to fall within the latter, many countries have now adopted an anti-discrimination policy framework, often (as in France, Germany, Spain, potentially Ireland) in addition to quota legislation. The focus of this anti-discrimination legislation has tended to be on employment retention and protection rather than promotion. Thornton and Lunt also found a general trend towards "the rhetoric of obligation rather than compulsion", towards the promotion of integration and the facilitation of the right to work.

This broad characterisation of policy frameworks is limited both in the impact of public policy on small and medium sized enterprises, which are often excluded from statutory obligations due to their size, and in terms of variations in applicability and implementation that exist at Member State level.

The 1997 publication also drew attention to the lack of discussion about quality of employment, stating that quota schemes are "not concerned with distribution of disabled employees throughout an organisation", their development and advancement. It is hoped that some of these issues are addressed in this report.

This chapter outlines definitions of disability and forms of action at Member State level, together with some information on the mediating organisations that assisted the study.

Definitions of Disability

Definitions of what constitutes a disability vary from country to country. Some Member States, such as France, the Netherlands and Spain, have defined a work disability. Other countries, such as Germany, Ireland and the United Kingdom, use a broader definition, largely based on the model defined by the World Health Organisation (WHO). The table below summarises the situation in each of the Member States studied.

Definitions of Disability

Member State	Definition of Disability
France	A disabled employee is defined as a person whose chances of obtaining or retaining a job are effectively restricted as a result of insufficient or reduced mental and physical capacities (Labour Code Art. L323-10) Under the Act of July 10, 1987 for the Promotion of the Employment of Disabled Workers, beneficiaries include persons recognised by COTOREP (see Glossary) as a 'disabled worker'; people with occupational accidents or diseases as a result of which they are in receipt of a pension; invalidity pension recipients; and military invalidity pension recipients and people in related categories.
Germany	A person with a disability is defined as any person affected by a functional impairment which is not merely temporary and which stems from a physical, mental or psychological condition which is not typical for the age of the person concerned (the WHO definition adopted in the Severely Disabled Persons Act ('Schwerbehindertengesetz'), 1974).People covered by the provisions of the Act must have a degree of disability defined on a scale as at least 50%. People defined as having a degree of 30% can apply to the employment service to be treated as having a severe disability with consequent rights. As the legislation stands, people who experience mental illness are not always recognised to have a severe disability.
Ireland	There is no statutory definition. The WHO definition is used by the Departments of Health and Social Welfare. A social model of disability used by state National Rehabilitation Board: "it is Irish society itself which disables and disadvantages its disabled citizens by means of its current structures, policies and practices."
Netherlands	A work disability is defined in terms of a person who, because of illness or deficiencies is not able, in appropriate employment, to earn the same amount as a healthy person with comparable education and experience (General Disability Act ('AAW') 1975, Art. 5). In addition to this definition, there is a broad definition of people with an incapacity for work selected on the basis of characteristics with can be objectively assessed (Work and Disabled Employees Act ('WAGW'), 1986. A number of Decrees have added to a 'safety net' category of employees covered by the financial support provisions of the WAGW who, "as a result of illness or impairment, suffer an unequivocal handicap in obtaining or performing work, or employees for whom special accommodation has been made to enable them to obtain or perform work".
Spain	A disabled worker is one affected by a reduction in physical and mental capacity to a degree not less than 33%, which prevents the person from finding and holding employment (Royal Decree 1445/1982).
United Kingdom	A person has a disability if he or she has a physical or mental impairment which has a substantial and long-term adverse effect on the ability to carry out normal day-to-day activities. The definition includes severe disfigurement; progressive conditions which do not yet have a substantial adverse effect; and past disabilities (Disability Discrimination Act).

Employment Protection Measures

Four of the Member States studied have specific measures in place to protect the rights of employees with disabilities. These measures are summarised in the table below.

Employment Protection Measures

Member State	Definition of Disability
France	Dismissal on the grounds of disability is prohibited, except where this can be justified in medically certified cases
Germany	Dismissal of an employee with a disability requires independent assessment and approval by a Central Welfare Office. The Office assesses the interests and views of both employer and employee before making a decision. The primary objective is always to maintain the employment relationship
Ireland	No specific protection measures
Netherlands	No specific protection measures
Spain	Employment discrimination is prohibited in the course of employment on the grounds of reductions in physical, psychological and sensory capabilities, as long as the person is able to perform the functions of their job (Social Integration of Disabled People Act, 1982)
United Kingdom	Employees with disabilities in firms of 20 or more employees have the legal right not to be treated less favourably on the grounds of their disability; employers are required to make reasonable adjustments to the workplace (Disability Discrimination Act)

Employment Promotion Measures

All Member States studied operate a range of employment protection measures. The nature of these differs from country to country, as does their enforcement and their applicability to small and medium sized enterprises.

In addition to these forms of employment promotion, every Member State operates a variety of financial assistance measures designed to promote the

Employment Promotion: Non-Financial Measures

Member State	Quota System	Other Non-Financial Measures
France	Target of 6% for companies employing 20 or more people; mandatory and enforced; several opt outs	It is illegal for employers to refuse employment on the grounds of an applicant's health or disability, or to exclude them from recruitment procedures unless the person's inability to carry out the job is medically certified.
Germany	Target of 6% for companies employing 16+ people; mandatory and enforced, with a compensatory levy of DM 200 for each post unfilled	Employers are obliged to assess whether vacancies that arise may be filled my people with disabilities
Ireland	Public sector 3%; voluntary, not enforced and not met	
Netherlands	Quota target of 5%; not implemented	Firms must consult with employment services when redundancies affecting people with disabilities are proposed.
Spain	Quota target of 2% for enterprises employing 50+ people; not enforced	Employment discrimination is prohibited (Social Integration of Disabled People Act, 1982)
United Kingdom	Un-enforced 3% quota abolished in 1995 with introduction of Disability Discrimination Act	

employment of people with disabilities. There is insufficient scope here to give detail to the variety of schemes found at national level although additional information can be found in the National Reports. However, two separate types of financial measure can broadly be distinguished: fixed rate incentives and variable rate facilitation measures.

Fixed rate incentives are designed to incentivise the employment of a person with a disability. they include:

- lump sum premiums linked to the signing of a permanent (indefinite term) contract, available in France, Spain;

- short or medium term employment subsidies, either at a flat rate or tapering off, that are normally linked to specific types of degrees of disability or specific intermediary organisations only, available in all Member States;

- discounts or exemptions from social insurance or other statutory charges, available in France, Ireland (short term, some forms of disability only), Spain.

Measures designed to facilitate new or continued employment are applied at variable rates linked to the nature of a disability and its impact on employment. These include:

- support to finance workplace adaptations, available in all Member States. These are subject to budgetary and/or fixed percentage restrictions in some Member States studied (such as Ireland and the United Kingdom);

- support for people with disabilities to attend interviews (including sign language interpretation) available in all Member States. These forms of support may not be linked to post-appointment support measures;

- long term wage subsidies at a level related to the degree of disability or support needs, available in most Member States. These tend to be available only under specific schemes or actions with strict eligibility criteria - they may not be widely available.

Chapter 4   The Case Studies

This chapter summarises each of the cases in the six Member States. For each country, a profile of the characteristics of the case studies is followed by a description of each case and issues arising. Descriptions of the mediating organisations and other agencies playing a role in the case studies are given in the Glossary.

France

Profile of French Case Studies

Business Characteristics

Case Studies	France 1	France 2	France 3
Trading activity	manufacturing	medical clinic	gastro-enterology clinic
Location	urban: northern Paris	urban: southern inner Paris	urban: southern Paris
Number of employees	6	25	5
Quota Scheme	Not applicable	Applicable	Not applicable

Characteristics of Employees with Disabilities

Case Studies	France 1	France 2	France 3
Number of employees	1	1	1
Gender	male	female	female
Age	not established	23	35
Type(s) of disability	not established	epilepsy, mobility	neurological and memory problems
Education attainments	not established	post-second level vocational training	second level
Job title/role	not established	receptionist/ switchboard operator	medical secretary
Employment status	new employee, within probationary period	two year temporary contract	permanent contract
Mediating organisation (see also Glossary)	Émergence	Émergence	Émergence

Case Study France 1: Manufacturing Company

Interviews were held with the employer and the Émergence placement agent.

The Enterprise

This enterprise is in a fiercely competitive market dominated by larger companies. At the same time, a fairly significant part of its production is entrusted to subcontractors. It operates under constant stress with an inflexible working rhythm. They have to meet customers' demands and adapt their procedures accordingly to survive. Given their small number, every employee is indispensable and has unique skills and duties.

The Employee

It was not possible to interview the employee. Neither the employer nor the placement agent were aware of the nature of his disability. Despite recognition by a COTOREP (see Glossary for definition) as having a Category A disability, the only clue was a wound on the employee's hand. The employer did not intend to enquire further. While he had expected to provide special facilities, there was no outward sign of disability and no measures had been necessary yet. As a result, no information about the disability had been passed on to the rest of his staff. The other employees regarded the recruit no differently to any other newcomer and no particular problems had ever been brought to the employer's attention.

Recruitment

The employer was looking for a versatile employee for circuitry work. He approached the national employment agency, ANPE, who had no suitable candidates. ANPE alerted Émergence. The employer required an employee with very specific skills. For him it was "a post to fill, end of story". While he felt that the image of disabled persons presented by the media bore no relation to the day-to-day reality of the workplace, the employee was taken on and is still undergoing an initial probationary period. The employer reserved final judgement but observed that the employee had done very well to date. Disabilities ruled out were those which impair people's independence and flexibility, and those which introduced an element of irregularity to the activity of the employee. It is not the severity of the disability that counts, he said, but its regularity.

Support Measures

Financial assistance in the form of a lump sum premium and other measures had come as a surprise to the employer. Émergence advised him and assisted in the application process. Despite this help, the forms were twice returned to the employer for amendment and he was critical about the assistance. Aid seemed to be accessible haphazardly, particularly as no action was taken to provide information on it. There was nothing to prevent an employer from abusing the system, terminating an employment contract after 12 months to start again with another beneficiary. Despite this, the amount allocated was felt unlikely to sway a decision. To this employer, a reduction of statutory social insurance contributions would have been preferable, allowing the advantage to be spread over the medium or long term. The volume of aid should also be proportionate to the severity of the disability.

Case Study France 2: Clinic
Interviews were held with the employer and the employee.

The Enterprise

This clinic is subject to the employment obligation (the 6% quota corresponding under the French system to 1.5 'beneficiary units', equivalent to a COTOREP-defined Category B ('moderate permanent') disability). The clinic therefore offered a post as receptionist and switchboard operator to a woman introduced by Émergence and recognised as having a disability by COTOREP. A specific feature of the clinic, partly because of its size, is the frequency with which emergencies occur. Employees work under great stress and are often overburdened. All are essential to their posts: it is difficult to replace any of them.

The Employee

This young woman, aged 23, was recruited in March 1996. In 1989 she received a vocational training certificate (CAP) in cold-meat sales. She worked in that sector for six months but she fell ill suddenly, with an acute neurological disorder (epilepsy with motor neurone imbalance, according to her employer). In 1990 she obtained recognition from COTOREP as in Category B. She attended an 18-month training course to receive a vocational training diploma (CAP-BEP) in administrative and commercial studies. She subsequently received jobseeking support from Émergence and took a one-year job on a work-and-welfare contract (CES) in a residents' association. The association was financially unable to renew the contract and she returned to Émergence. The employee says that her condition does not cause her any trouble in everyday life. The employee has no problems with the job, her performance is good and her disability is not known to the rest of the staff. She was gratified that there were no signs of absenteeism. However, according to her employer, she has experienced some integration difficulties, is slightly depressive, and has sometimes been on the brink of a seizure, reassured by the presence of doctors. She also commented that managing employees with disabilities occasionally took time and greater attentiveness. The employee was more motivated than other employees and, being unmarried, was better able to cope with the constraints of an occupation in which working hours were often determined by sudden emergencies. The employee seems satisfied with her work.

Recruitment

The employee was recruited as the result of a request made to Émergence by the manager of the clinic. While the board of the parent company was not in favour of her appointment, due to her disability, she successfully defended her decision. The employee competed for selection with other candidates, both disabled and non-disabled, and was chosen on the basis of her interview, qualifications and motivation. The employee has a two-year temporary contract, earning the statutory minimum wage, and was awarded a premium of FF 10,000 on recruitment. For the manager, who had experience of employing a person with a disability from a previous job, physical appearance is the most important factor in determining whether an applicant with a disability would be taken on: clients are in an anxious frame of mind and visible disabilities would be very difficult to handle.

Support Measures

COTOREP recognition and the quota played a part in this decision making process. The enterprise received a recruitment premium (FF 10,000 on signature of the contract, following acceptance by AGEFIPH, FF 5,000 at the end of one year, exemption from the entire employer's social security contribution for two years, and a monthly allowance of FF 2,000. Payment of the premium was taking a long time. The support available meant that the employee cost barely half as much as any other employee.

Case Study France 3: Gastro-enterology Centre

Interviews were held with the employer and the employee.

The Enterprise

This enterprise is located in a clinic which is not very accessible to people with reduced mobility, the main entrance is at the top of a long staircase. It is a very new enterprise, not subject to the quota, and the recruitment of a person recognised by COTOREP has enabled it to staff its reception desk all day at reduced cost. The employer reiterated previous arguments about the need for a sustained working rhythm and consistent availability. Being indispensable is more gratifying and motivating to the employee.

The Employee

This employee is a young woman of 35, the victim of a car accident who emerged from a coma with enormous memory problems and other neurological disorders. The accident occurred shortly after the young woman had passed her final school examinations, the Baccalauréate. When she awoke from the coma, she did not recognise her family, had no idea about her past and had to assimilate everything she was told about her previous life. She received no psychological or psychomotor aftercare. On leaving the hospital she was disorientated. She resumed her studies, matriculating for the first year of a degree course in law, but gradually became aware that she was unable to follow the classes. Moreover, she had huge problems with orientation and balance in addition to her memory problems. A state of depression set in about a year after her release from hospital. The employee stated that earlier intervention was needed.

Most of the rehabilitation courses on offer relate largely to manual tasks, and vocational certificates, with nothing at university entrance level. After abandoning law, she tried to study business management. In 1983, she gave up and applied to COTOREP for recognition of her status. With this she attended a course for middle management work in hospitals. However, the level of instruction was quite low; "they treated us as if we were mentally handicapped," and for potential employers the diploma issued had no value.

Between 1987 and 1992 she took a permanent contract as a secretary in a DIY supermarket chain. Following this, she attended a course in accountancy, worked part-time for a while, but only found odd jobs and temporary work. She could only obtain work-and-welfare contracts (CES), because she had not been unemployed long enough to qualify for priority treatment. She then tried to find work in the Paris region by placing newspaper advertisements, a common method in France. She did not mention her disability: employers, she believed, regard such people as more delicate, as having some kind of mental weakness.

No real interviews materialised. She approached a body specialising in finding jobs for the people with disabilities. She was then offered a three-month period of work experience, from July to September 1996 in the clinic in case France 2 with her progress monitored by Émergence. She completed this successfully and her name was put forward in October 1996 for employment in this gastro-enterology centre.

The employee believes that her disability is expressed in a lack of self-confidence. She says she is tense and overemotional, and ascribes this to the absence of psychological aftercare when she came out of hospital. She also tires very quickly. At work, she believes she is slower than anyone else due to her motor and co-ordination problems. Her greatest motivating factor is having a salary but it is also an interesting job. She believes it is better to work within a small structure than a large business, provided that the staff get on with each other.

Her employer believes that her level of education and general knowledge enable her to adapt well. She has become well integrated, but is never "in top form". She is very reliable and never guilty of absenteeism. She uses computers without problems but does not understand everything she does. Her daily routine involves collaboration with administrative and nursing staff working in the clinic where the centre is based and with the doctors who use the centre. The other employees of the centre, and the clinic in which it is located, know that she had an accident but have been sympathetic. She has to be monitored because of her memory problems, which demands work and vigilance on the part of her employer, but there is a good working atmosphere and the arrangement works well. Moreover, her family has played a supportive role.

Recruitment

The recruitment of the employee with a disability was largely determined by the previous job of the employer, who had previously been on the secretarial staff of a body specialising in the professional integration of people with disabilities. The employer took it for granted that the employment of people with disabilities is a normal collective responsibility and a natural primary duty of employers. The procedure followed was identical to that for the clinic in case France 2, although here the contract was permanent. As in that case, employees with more generally visible disabilities would not be desirable.

Support Measures

Financial assistance was crucial to this new business. As in case France 2, this employee will cost half the normal amount to employ for almost two years. This may be decisive as the business builds up its clientele.

Germany

Profile of German Case Studies

Business Characteristics

Characteristics of Employees with Disabilities

Case Studies	Germany 1	Germany 2	Germany 3
Trading activity	care for the elderly and ill	construction engineering	manufacturing
Established	1988	Not established	
Location	urban: North Rhine-Westphalia	urban: North Rhine-Westphalia	urban: North Rhine-Westphalia
Number of employees	170 (50 full time) nationally; branch 80% female	5; 4 full time, 1 part time	6 full time; 5 men, 1 woman (the employer's partner)
Quota Scheme	Applicable	Not applicable	Not applicable

Case Study Germany 1: Domiciliary Care

Case Studies	Germany 1	Germany 2	Germany 3
Number of employees	1	1	1
Gender	female	male	male
Age	30;	middle age	24
Type(s) of disability	muscular disease	mental illness	learning disability
Education attainments	second level	second level, vocational training	special schooling
Job title/role	accounts clerk	draftsman	factory operative
Employment status	full time	part time (30 hours/week)	full time, subsidised
Mediating organisation (see also Glossary)	Arbeitsamt (employment office); Fürsorgestelle (welfare office)	None	Workshop for people with learning disabilities

Interviews were held with the employee, the employer, a supervisor, works council official, a work colleague, occupational doctor/ergonomist and representatives of the employment and welfare offices.

The Enterprise

The enterprise, which provides domiciliary care for the elderly and the sick, started life as a sort of self-help organisation. The service is unusual in that it includes basic care, medical treatment and meals. The company was given a boost with the introduction of statutory care insurance. The staff are mainly qualified medical or geriatric nurses, with a number of semi-skilled nursing auxiliaries and people doing community service instead of military service. They are paid the normal wages for the sector, are relatively young and recruited locally. Both management and staff regard the workforce as highly motivated, and staff turnover is considerably below the sectoral average. All the firm's full-time staff and most of its part-time staff have permanent contracts and there is a compulsory works council. Many of the employees have regular clients, work independently and visit offices only for regular co-ordination meetings and to collect supplies. There is also a small task force for emergencies and unexpected staff shortages. In addition, all the employees interviewed felt it important to make jobs available for people with disabilities, since in a way they earned their living from the fact that other people needed help.

Seven people with disabilities are employed. At the main branch these include one person with cerebral palsy, one with quadriplegia, one with a disability that was not established and the case study employee: a woman with a muscular disease who works in the wages and accounts unit.

The Employee

The employee has restricted movement as a result of the muscular disease and cannot walk or stand for long periods. She spends most of the day in a wheelchair, but needs to walk at regular intervals for therapeutic reasons. After leaving secondary school (when still in good health) she trained as a clerk in a car supplies firm. Following the onset of the disease she continued working in this company, doing computerised wage accounting. The company went bankrupt in 1991. While unemployed, she applied to more than 200 firms without success and would have taken "any work". Her present job is in line with her training and gives her great satisfaction. She feels that she works very hard not just to make up for her incapacity, but also to make herself as "indispensable" as possible.

Recruitment

When the previous wages and accounts worker was to leave, the employer approached the local employment office as usual. The office was unable to provide a suitable applicant. Some information was held on the future employee in their files, but this was incomplete and the placement officer was unable to interpret them correctly. By chance the mediator from the local welfare office was able to put the employee forward for the job. The employer considered her expertise to be suitable and arranged an interview. He asked for more detailed information on her basic capability and required an independent medical assessment. A number of changes were made to the employee's workstation as a result of a separate ergonomic inspection, these were amended by the employer (who chose lower cost solutions) and 80% funded by the welfare office. The employee fitted in well, working both independently and full-time under a flexitime system. At the end of her probationary period she was confirmed in her post.

The employer showed a strong sense of social responsibility but employees had to fit into the firm. Impaired performance was accepted and compensated for, but he expected people to be motivated and to want to work. He tried to ensure that their jobs were as interesting and demanding as possible.

Events did not always work as smoothly as in this case. The firm had first employed disabled workers six years previously. After some initially positive experiences there were three cases where the workers were discovered to be not suitable only after the probationary period expired. The firm successfully negotiated their dismissal with the central welfare office, due to general misconduct and poor performance. He felt that the employment and welfare offices were glad to place people regardless of their compatibility with the employer. The conciliation part of the procedure had, in one case, led to an unpleasant working atmosphere and difficulties establishing proof. It had been suggested that he had not come up with "any good ideas" for changes to work organisation, as if it was assumed that another job could be created specially. In one instance the procedure had taken over six months. There were no problems with the worker who had then taken the post, also disabled.

The employment quota was no longer a factor in recruitment, as the firm had already more than filled it. The quota would never be the sole reason for recruitment. Employees with disabilities had usually placed an increased burden on the company through absence arising from their disability. Nor was there always easy justification in economic terms. The man with cerebral palsy had actual productivity level of around 50%. Despite this, he was highly motivated and a hard worker, a bonus for the firm.

The employer found the mediators sometimes very slow and laborious, with a bureaucratic mentality, changes of staff and some incompetence. The interviewee from the local welfare office was critical of the employment authorities and - because of what she regarded as some badly handled dismissals - of the employer.

Case Study Germany 2: Engineering Consultancy
Interviews were held with the employee, the employer, supervisor and the employment and welfare offices.

The Enterprise
This construction engineering consultancy employs four people on permanent contracts and one temporary. A particular feature of the work of this enterprise is that it tends to have short deadlines. The work is difficult to plan as it often

involves ad-hoc requirements which have to be met for the company to secure business. The wages paid, including to the employee who is mentally ill, are above the nationally-agreed levels, the owner regards this as important so as not to lose staff to other firms. He is also deadline oriented rather than work hours oriented. Employees can take time off during normal work hours for private reasons if required and make it up elsewhere. The employer set great store by having a good working atmosphere and stated that he has no preconceptions about disability.

The Employee

This employee with a disability became mentally ill as a result of depression. He is classified by the employment office as "equivalent to disabled", since he would be given a disability rating of 100 if he applied for a disability pass. He studied as a structural engineer and then worked as the self-employed head of an office producing construction drawings. The permanent pressure of deadlines and the uncertain supply of work placed him under severe pressure, which led to his illness. He did not plan to give up work, which he saw as an essential factor in promoting his recovery and a return to an independent life. His work in the firm is organised such that he liases solely with his employer and colleagues do not have to make allowances for his disability in their work. Despite this, the atmosphere in the enterprise is good and disability is among the topics discussed openly. The employee sees this as an advantage as he is not under pressure to conceal his illness. The employer has also defined strategies for managing the employee's illness, including ways of shielding him from pressure and supporting him to find solutions when flustered. These were not quantified as an extra burden.

Recruitment

The employee took on a new job, created out of part of the employer's own tasks which were previously often subcontracted: producing drawings and structural analyses for construction projects. The employer was not subject to the employment quota and had no plans to recruit a person with a disability. He advertised the post and the employee-to-be applied. He was interviewed on the strength of his application. Samples of his work made a strong impression. At the interview he also talked about his mental illness, what it involved and his continuing treatment. The firm does not have a policy when it comes to recruitment, although fitting in is as important as ability. The owner of the firm had no previous experience or information regarding depression, but the applicant's qualifications matched the job profile, he liked him and so decided to take him on. The employee had to be independent with the disability having no impact upon his performance. The employer assumed that his ability would become clear during the probationary period. During this period the employer investigated the illness, but this did not influence his decision and the employee was kept on even when the assistance payments ended.

The official from the welfare office regards his appointment as an extraordinary stroke of luck. The applicant went through the normal application procedure and was successful. If, however, there had been another applicant who had seemed equally suitable, this might not have happened.

Support Measures

The employee advised the employer about the possibility of an allowance and the employer approached the employment office. The procedure was described as uncomplicated which had surprised him. He was granted an allowance, but would have taken the worker on even without it.

The employer felt that, to make the quota persuasive, the compensatory levy should be high enough to make it a genuine incentive or adequate financial assistance should be provided. Financial assistance should distinguish between different types and degrees of disability, permanent financial support in cases of permanent underperformance.

Case Study Germany 3: Manufacturing Company

Interviews were held with the employer, foreman, a work colleague and the mediating organisation (2).

The Enterprise

This enterprise produces industrial extraction units and industrial boilers, largely on a one-off basis, manufactured by hand without the use of much machinery. All six full-time employees are on permanent contracts and are responsible for production management. The owner acts in a supervisory capacity and as sales representative. His wife does the clerical work. What counts for the success of the business is the quality of the goods it produces and the owner's personal contacts with his customers. The firm faces little local competition in the production of extraction units, but the company is facing new constraints in the form of EU Directives on standards. This is likely to lead to high costs and rationalisation.

The owner promotes good relations between employees avoiding giving any preferential treatment to individuals. Most of the staff have been with the firm since it was founded.

The employer has two sons, both of whom have learning disabilities. While they have found a job for the elder son, the family had never considered the possibility of employing them in the firm because they feared it would be resented by the staff.

The Employee

The employee has severe learning difficulties and is categorised as having a degree of disability of 100. He needs to be retaught any new activities which he learns but which are then not practised for some time. He has an inability to concentrate and a limited attention span. Nevertheless he is motivated, very willing to learn, and he is able to perform the tasks he is assigned to the employer's satisfaction. He has a back injury which rules out any heavy physical work.

He has not had any vocational training and had never had a job in a firm on the regular labour market. He had learnt small-scale craft activities such as making wooden toys, and had practised working with tools. It was not clear initially what tasks he would be able to do, so started by helping out. However, it was important to exploit his potential to the full, both for economic reasons and to ensure his successful integration and well-being.

He was assigned a mentor, initially the foreman but subsequently another employee with more patience. The staff were initially sceptical but their reservations were overcome. The employee gradually began to work in all areas of production. He was always given clearly defined tasks to determine what he was able to do and how much instruction he needed. Training and intensive supervision were unavoidable. Over time he proved to be capable of doing welding, painting and cutting, and his productivity has increased. The types of tasks he performs are fairly limited, and he is hardly ever asked to do anything new which would involve further training. His performance cannot be classified as economically efficient. There is insufficient demand for only the tasks that he can do well. Since these do not make up a full-time job in a small company, he is repeatedly required to work in areas where he is not so capable or needs a lot of instruction.

Recruitment

The idea of employing a disabled worker first came from the manager of a workshop for people with disabilities who is a friend of the employer's family and knows his personal circumstances and the situation in the firm. This manager was aware of the job possibility and, after finding out what the job involved, suggested the future employee. The manager felt that the person could do the job, and the owner knew how to deal with his disability and would help to integrate him into the firm. The enterprise was not required to fill an employment quota. The owner was still unsure and the idea was discussed with the staff in advance. All agreed, but pointed out their lack of experience. They were not given any training or preparation, however.

Support Measures

100% financial support was provided for the first three years and whether the recruit would have been given the job without this initial assistance is questionable. According to the employer, a job for someone with this disability will always need to be subsidised to be economically viable and 100% assistance was justified. Nevertheless he intended to keep the employee on once the assistance provided came to an end. During his employment, the employer would be reluctant to take on a second person with a disability. His experience made him feel that only jobs involving easy tasks were suitable for such employees, but many of these were being scrapped.

The employer criticised the limited contact that officials from the welfare office had with him once the early stages of the employment period were over. The employee's performance had on one occasion inexplicably dropped, but the employer had been reluctant to talk to anyone at the welfare office without there being a regular opportunity for contact.

Ireland

Profile of Irish Case Studies

Business Characteristics

Case Studies	Ireland 1	Ireland 2	Ireland 3	Ireland 4
Trading activity	electrical switch gear manufacture	contract cleaning and grounds maintenance	lighting and plastics manufacture	bakery and food manufacture
Established	c. 1971	1996	c. 1966	c. 1946
Location	rural: Co. Kildare, small town	urban: Co. Dublin	urban: Co. Dublin	urban: Co. Dublin
Number and gender of employees	50 total; 46 male, 4 female	19 total; 12 male, 7 female	60 total; 49 male, 11 female	70 total; 60 male, 10 female

Characteristics of Employees with Disabilities

Case Studies	Ireland 1	Ireland 2	Ireland 3	Ireland 4
Number of employees	1	2	1	2
Gender	male	male	male	1 female, 1 male
Age	24	31; 38	35	n/known; 22
Type(s) of disability	learning disability and slight physical disability	learning disability	mental illness	1 learning disability; 1 epilepsy
Education attainments	basic second level schooling: no leaving certificate	both have basic second level schooling and vocational training	third level qualifications (graduated prior to diagnosis)	special school; basic second level. Both with vocational training
Job title/role	factory operative	1 cleaner; 1 gardener	Planner/ Programmer	bakery operatives
Employment status	initially part time, now full time permanent	full time, permanent, paid benefits plus top-up	full time, temporary/ probationary, subsidised	full time, permanent, one post 40% subsidised
Mediating organisation (see also Glossary)	National Rehab. Board (NRB)	STEP Enterprises	Worklink, Schizophrenia Ireland	Rehab

Case Study Ireland 1: Electrical Products Manufacturer

Interviews were held with the employee, a manager and supervisor. An interview was not possible with the trade union representative.

The Enterprise

This firm is involved in the manufacture of electrical switch gear. Most staff are employed on a permanent basis, after 13 weeks trial period. This year, due to increased demand, they took on a number of temporary staff on 6 month contracts with no pension or sick pay. The company is implementing a staff pension plan gives bonuses a few times each year. The company gets very few applications from women, their recruitment on the factory floor would need the introduction of new toilet facilities. Existing facilities are not wheelchair accessible.

The Employee with a Disability

This employee has a slight co-ordination problem and a learning disability. He left school at 17 years old and, apart from six months' unemployment, has been working since. Most previous jobs were work experience placements, two in manufacturing. He heard about the vacancy for a factory worker through KARE, a mediating agency, about eighteen months ago. He was recruited first on a part-time and then a full-time basis. This led to him losing his entitlement to state benefits, a major risk. His decision was informed and supported by his mediators. There was a need for more intensive supervisory input at the beginning of the job, although this has now eased.

The employment of a previous employee with a learning disability ended after a trial period because of lapses in concentration that were a safety hazard. A second previous employee who had co-ordination problems and a slight learning disability found it hard to integrate with other staff. These same concerns were considered with the current employee. KARE has assisted integration, partly by taking a holistic view of his welfare, rather than a narrow view of his work role.

Recruitment

The company does not engage in a proactive recruitment programme as there is high demand from the local town and they have low turnover. The Production Manager is responsible for the recruitment of all factory floor staff although, in the case of the employees with a disability, the Managing Director made the decision. An official job application form is used which specifically mentions disability. The company has not previously requested a medical examination of candidates, but is about to introduce one, to test hearing and eyesight and establish a baseline in case of litigation for damage in the workplace. The company concern is to recruit people with the best skills. High value is placed on good personal skills and motivation. Employees need to be physically fit to do the work.

There are no independent applications from people with disabilities, nor were there recently any from women. The previous employees with disabilities were also recruited through KARE who approached the Managing Director. KARE enabled the company to take them on at no initial cost. After one year, the company paid a full salary to the employee but was refunded 60%. KARE was positively viewed for their selections and support. If a person with a disability came directly to the company with no support from a mediating agency, the company would have to consider safety issues, in particular, carefully. Where a job was affected by a disability, a different job would be offered if there was a vacancy. There are no contractual differences for employees with disabilities.

The personal motivation of the Managing Director was an important factor in the decision to recruit people with disabilities. He had no personal experience of disability but wanted to do something to promote equal opportunities for this group. The absence of financial risk was also seen as important, but there was a conscious understanding of the potential for mutual benefit. The interviewees felt that one of the best ways to overcome the concerns and prejudices of employers is to involve employers with successful examples of integration in the process.

Case Study Ireland 2: Contract Cleaning and Gardening

Interviews were held with the two employees with disabilities and the employer.

The Enterprise

The new enterprise provides maintenance, mobile cleaning and janitor services to property management companies. All employees are on eleven month contracts, with basic entitlements. The contracts are renewable and, after two years, employees will be taken on permanently. They work a 39 hour week. There is no sick leave available. The company has no union representation. The employer previously worked for STEP Enterprises, a training and placement agency for people with disabilities, for over seven years.

The Employees

The company presently has two employees with disabilities, both with a learning disability. Their contracts are both permanent, they work a full week and are in receipt of a state benefit. As a result, they receive a low sum which is the maximum that they are allowed to earn without losing their entitlement. Both employees came from STEP Enterprises.

The first employee is aged 31 and works in the contract cleaning section. He also drives the company van to take the other cleaners to their places of work. His driving licence was obtained through STEP. He has access to the van for personal use as an incentive, and he does gardening work once a week. He has been with the company since it started. He left school with no qualifications and went straight into STEP Enterprises. He lacked confidence to look elsewhere for work. STEP arranged work experience for him in a small firm making fishing tackle. He left this job when he received burns to his arms, making lead weights without protective gloves, and returned to STEP. The company owner offered him the job when he set up the company. He still has a job coach from STEP. The employee aims to come off benefit but the employer is doubtful about his earnings potential.

The second employee is aged 38 and works in gardening and grounds maintenance. He left school early with no qualifications. He joined a sheltered employment agency where he made school bags, then moved to STEP where he was trained and worked in his current role. He joined the new company in February 1996. He had not applied for work himself as he feared going outside sheltered employment and mixing with people. He has no job coach. This case study is exceptional in that the owner has a long history of working with people with disabilities. His commitment is recognised by both employees who felt that they could approach him for help and be confident of receiving it.

Recruitment

There is no formal recruitment policy and the employer does not use application forms. Applicants contact the company and are called in for interview. The company does not require a medical examination but does require Garda (police) clearance, as work involves access to people's homes. Most recruitment is through state employment agencies and agencies supporting people with disabilities. As this is a new company, the owner aimed to reduce costs in the first few years by employing unemployed people under a 'Back to Work Scheme' whereby employers' costs are reduced, the employee retains 75% of their unemployment assistance, all associated benefits for three years and, in addition, gets a wage from the company.

Placement and support agencies for people with disabilities typically ask him to employ people on a few months' work experience. The company has employed five people with disabilities. Each of three women who took placements had experienced head injuries. They were paid an allowance by Headway and supported by job coaches. Each found it tough work, were married with children and stated to be under pressure to be at home. They stayed for only one or two months.

The owner stressed that it is his desire to continue to work with people with disabilities that motivates him rather than any financial incentive. He has lower output expectations of people with disabilities and puts less pressure on them than on other employees. While the financial cost of employing people with disabilities is low, the cost in terms of management and supervision can be high.

Employees with disabilities were stated to need more supervision, an extra demand on his time. Some previous employees also had a lack of personal initiative causing difficulties with supervision. The owner felt that most supervisors would prefer not to work with people with disabilities. He believes that his employees do not need much additional support from outside agencies as he can provide support himself.

Nevertheless, it would be difficult for his company to compete on the open market with training agencies who provide the same service while in receipt of a high level of subsidy. While the pay received by employees is low due to the rules attached to their benefits, they could not be paid a full wage for less than full productivity. The enterprise could pay more and offer incentives such as overtime if the benefits earnings disregard were higher. One employee is aware that the only way that he can increase his earning power is also by increasing his insecurity. The employer questioned why he should not have the same status as a long term unemployed person, and qualify for the Back to Work Scheme. A direct subsidy to the employer for supervision might also be an equitable and effective way of encouraging integration, based on the nature and extent of supervision needed.

Case Study Ireland 3: Plastics Manufacturer

Interviews were held with the employee (2) a manager and a Trade Union representative (to whom the identity of the employee was not revealed).

The Enterprise

This company manufactures glass and plastic products. Employees working in administration (except for one person with a disability) are salaried while production workers receive the same hourly rate of pay. There is a sick pay scheme. The budget for staff is worked out annually, at which time it is decided whether or not to renew temporary contracts. The whole factory is on the ground floor but is not fully wheelchair accessible.

The Employee

The company currently employs one person with a disability, aged 35 years with a degree in Production Engineering and a Diploma in Computer Science. He is on a twelve month contract, taken on nine months ago, employed under a programme not specifically designed for people with a disability. Under the programme, the company pays 50% of his salary while Forbairt, a state agency, pays the remainder and a grant for technology training courses (the procedure for accessing training funds is seen as overly bureaucratic). The employee was diagnosed as suffering from schizophrenia at the end of 1991. He left a good permanent job in England in 1990 and worked temporarily in London until his family brought him home. After diagnosis he took two contract jobs but, on the second, his medication was not correct and his work was affected. He then completed a course with Worklink, a mediating agency, and was placed as a Planner/Programmer in the company following an interview with the Operations Manager. Only those working closest to him know of his diagnosis, but the employee is unaware of this.

His job is a new one. The company created a vacancy just as he was made known to them. He has completed his initial task (adapting a computer programme) well and is now responsible for programming work schedules and assessing actual hours spent on jobs. The Operations Manager hopes to renew his contract when up for renewal. To do this he will have to justify to the Managing Director that he is still required, even though his original task is over. The manager had hoped that the employee would integrate better to increase his chances of being kept on, and believed that more personal support would have assisted this.

The employee's only state benefit is a medical card which he is about to lose and he will now have to pay for drug costs up to IR£30 per month. These costs are an additional burden associated with managing a disability and are not incurred by non-disabled people doing the same work for the same pay.

Recruitment

The company does not have a specific policy regarding the recruitment of people with disabilities. Their general recruitment policy is to first advertise vacancies internally at the behest of the union in the company. The selection procedure involves completing an application form, a first interview with the Head of Department then a second with the Managing Director. The company has not required medical examinations, but like the enterprise in case Ireland 1, shall shortly be introducing one at the insistence of the company's insurer. The Operations Manager believes that this new insistence is inspired by new Health and Safety Legislation. The focus is mostly on testing employees' hearing as ear protection is required on the factory floor.

The Operations Manager was not aware of any people with disabilities applying directly for work. Nor do many women apply for the factory work. The company employed no-one with a disability before he came to the company six years ago. Since then, he has taken on two people with disabilities, one for work experience. Both were taken as the result of an approach by agencies working with people with disabilities, Worklink, the training wing of Schizophrenia Ireland, and STEP Enterprises. The Operations Manager has a personal connection with Worklink: his wife was involved in setting up Worklink. They have family experience of schizophrenia and he wished to help in some way. His personal experience also helped him allay the fears of staff members.

The person previously employed had multiple disabilities. The company was not a safe environment for him and he was also subject to sniggering and whispering by a few co-workers due to his poor speech. The placement was discontinued. The Manager thought that there may be additional barriers facing women with disabilities in this case. They would probably have to work in the clerical or sales side and, if it were a choice between two equal candidates, one with a disability and one without, he feared that the person without the disability would get it. The risk perceived might override their value.

To the employee, his main recruitment problem is the gaps in his CV that he can only explain by reference to his illness. There is a powerful stigma attached to schizophrenia in Ireland. Mention of his illness to one employment agency put them off and it is no longer referred to, leaving no explanation. One advantage of the agency route, however, is that they do not use application forms and a form is only completed at interview stage. It is only then that he has to account for his work history.

Neither the Manager nor the employee were aware of other schemes available to facilitate the employment of people with disabilities. The Manager felt that tax allowances could provide an important incentive for companies as a way of compensating for any reduced productivity, graded according to the degree of the severity of the disability. The assistant shop steward, when interviewed, was unaware of the union's policy regarding disability.

Case Study Ireland 4: Bakery
Interviews were held with the two employees and a manager.

The Enterprise
All bakery factory floor workers are entitled to the statutory entitlements. Sick pay operates on the basis of a doctor's note after three days absence. Starting pay is about £140 per week, reviewed annually. The working environment is not accessible for wheelchair users.

The Employees
There are currently two employees with disabilities working for the company both of whom work on the factory floor. Both were recruited through NTDI, a mediating organisation. The first employee suffers from epilepsy. He completed his schooling to age 16 then completed a three month NTDI multi-skills course, some training in engineering and a three month work experience placement. He only applied for 3 or 4 jobs when he was in the Training Centre. He thought his

chances were not good due to his disability. His epilepsy is under control, although he does not receive warnings of seizures. His pay is subsidised to 40%. The second employee has a slight learning disability. She is not necessarily as fast as others in her work. The response has been to give her tasks where she can work well to her own speed so that her performance is equal to that of other staff in the same job. There is no subsidy. She attended a 'Special School' until she was aged 18 then took a three year catering course. Her supervisor told her about work experience at the bakery after which she was taken on.

Recruitment

The General Manager and the Production Manager are responsible for recruitment. The bakery normally approach FÁS, the state training agency, or NTDI. They attempt to employ locally as the hours are difficult. The General Manager short-lists candidates based on age, previous experience and previous wage. The company prefers candidates in their late teens/early twenties with some experience in the food industry. Both managers interview candidates where possible. They are about to formalise procedures through an application form, induction programme and employee handbooks. There is no medical examination of candidates but questions about health are important due to food allergies. Production line vacancies need to be filled quickly, the temptation is to go for quick solutions and there is scope for mediating agencies to become more proactive.

The company does not have a specific policy regarding the recruitment of people with a disability, but they are actively involved with NTDI. This happened by chance through a business connection. Their experience has been good from the beginning, an experience mirrored by the employees. The company has employed six people with disabilities and all were recruited through NTDI. No one with a disability has ever applied directly for work on their own behalf. The practice of employing people with a disability is driven by the General Manager: some members of his family have epilepsy and he believes that disability should not be a barrier to employment. The Manager believes that people with a disability tend to have more motivation and commitment, and appreciate the opportunity to work. Wage subsidisation is not a major factor. Some of the six employees with disabilities were subsidised but others were not. While all six worked well, the company relocated and the new premises were no longer convenient for four of them. At least one has found work in another bakery.

According to the General Manager, the agency was professional in identifying both the potential and the limitations of all six candidates, which made the integration process fairly easy. Their support is a crucial factor for both employer and employee. Despite a supportive environment, there were sometimes examples of harassment from fellow workers: sometimes the disability being blamed for accidents that were not the person's fault; other times, more general 'slagging'. The General Manager had limited awareness of support schemes and funds for workplace adaptation. However, according to this employer, broader public awareness is even more important.

The Netherlands

Profile of Dutch Case Studies

Business Characteristics

Case Studies	Netherlands 1	Netherlands 2	Netherlands 3
Trading activity	nursing home	specialised cleaning services	healthcare: rehabilitation foundation
Location	rural; village community in eastern Netherlands	rural; provincial town	urban: town in Randstad
Number and gender of employees	120	20, plus circa 150 on call	5, plus 7 voluntary posts

Characteristics of Employees with Disabilities

Case Studies	Netherlands 1	Netherlands 2	Netherlands 3
Number of employees	1	1	1
Gender	female	female	male
Age	34	30	38
Type(s) of disability	mobility disability	mobility disability	mental illness
Education attainments	basic second level	basic second level	third level
Job title/role	Receptionist/ Telephonist	Clerical assistant (wages dept)	project worker, on 9 month project
Employment status	part time, permanent	full time, permanent	part time, temporary
Mediating organisation (see also Glossary)	none directly	GAK Detapool	Bedrijfsverenigingen (Industrial Insurance Boards)

Case Study Netherlands 1: Nursing Home

Interviews were held with the employee, the previous director of the enterprise and the current head of personnel.

The Enterprise

The company provides temporary or permanent nursing and rehabilitation for bedridden patients. It is an independent institution located in a rural village community in the east of the Netherlands. Due to the nature of the service, the premises are fully accessible for wheelchair users.

The Employee

The employee was born in 1962. Her educational attainments comprise a few years of MAVO (lower secondary education) with no diploma due to bronchitis and a moped accident. From the age of seventeen, not yet disabled, she had short periods of employment interspersed with unemployment. Her jobs including retail checkout operator and sales assistant, metal processing factory worker, hospital cleaner/ancillary worker. She was dismissed during the trial period in her last retail job (late 1980), probably due to frequent absence with bronchitis. In a car accident in early 1981 she suffered a spinal cord lesion in her midriff. She is confined to a wheelchair and cannot stand or walk. Her rehabilitation ended in late 1981 and she joined the enterprise in January 1982. She works as receptionist/telephonist in a group of 6 female receptionists.

Her working hours have increased over the course of her employment. From 1991 onwards she has worked two days of 3 hours plus two days of 6 hours plus weekend duty every three weeks. In 1985 the employee began to experience difficulties in coping with psychological problems connected with her traffic accident and she was on sick leave for nearly a year. She felt that her employer provided inadequate support then due to limited contact. Despite this, she refused a full WAO disability benefit and returned to work within a year. She is currently in receipt of a full WAO benefit as a result of illness.

Recruitment

A friend of the employee knew that there would be a temporary job available in the nursing home where she worked, during a colleague's maternity leave. She spoke to the director about her friend applying for the job. The director suggested she write in, which she did. The director had no other candidates in mind and, in inviting the application, was likely to take her on. She was called for a short and informal interview, where she spoke of her fears about the reactions of visitors to her disability, but the director was able to reassure her.

While no medical examination took place, adjustments to the workplace were discussed internally with an in-house ergotherapist. Her friend showed her around and taught her the job in her free time during the two months prior to commencement. The job was initially temporary but subsequently became permanent.

The director's reasons for taking the employee related to the small size and supportiveness of the local community. He had heard about her accident and was willing to help her. The social policy of the nursing home extends to employment matters. The former director stated that "As carers, our responsibility should not stop with the patients and residents in the home, but should also extend to care for the staff working for us." Not all management and staff supported the decision initially: some managers wanted staff who were 100% deployable, other staff were affected by changes to working hours or routines (for example, to cover the time it took for her to use the toilet). The introduction of more flexibility in working hours when the employee was recruited was a deliberate action by the director. In the beginning, visitors and some staff tended to see her as a patient rather than a staff member. Negative attitudes disappeared over time with familiarity, however, and there is a good working atmosphere.

The employee believes that the 1981 Year of the Disabled focused more attention on the possibility of employing people with a disability. In addition, a 5% employment quota was introduced during the recruitment period under the WAGW (law on employment of people with disabilities). Despite its non-implementation, it may also have had an impact. The fact that hardly any adjustments had to be made to the premises made the decision to recruit her easier. The same is true of the presence of an ergotherapist and a rehabilitation specialist.

Support Measures

For the first six months the employee was taken to work by friends, neighbours and family members. Once she passed her driving test, a specially adapted car was allocated to her by the Industrial Insurance Board. She was granted her own parking place next to the main entrance of the home. In 1996 a Board ergonomist prescribed a covered parking place which could be heated, but this was not be in line with the architectural norms of the local council planning committee and could not be implemented. The problem was solved when it was discovered that the employee could apply for a minibus from the Board which she could ride into on her wheelchair with no need to cover over her parking space. Her application for the minibus has recently been approved.

In 1994 she began to have trouble with her back. The in-house ergotherapist advised her to obtain a better wheelchair and she started up the application procedure with the Board for a better wheelchair due to back problems. This proved to be a lengthy, bureaucratic and problematic procedure, during which her back trouble worsened. This, and the emotional problems it entailed, led again to illness and absence. At the beginning of 1996, a Board ergonomist recommended a wheelchair which was provided in late 1996, but the rehabilitation specialist at the nursing home declared that the back rest was unsuitable and a new application had to be submitted. The employee is now on full WAO benefit and working as a form of occupational therapy.

The employer lost out because the authorities providing the facilities did not perform properly. The employee has been supported by the chair of the national WAO Platform to deal with these problems. She believes that the situations could have been avoided if a budget had been made available to her to select a suitable wheelchair herself.

Case Study Netherlands 2: Specialised Cleaning Company

Interviews were held with the employee, the company director and the mediator.

The Enterprise

This enterprise provides specialised and extensive cleaning operations in planned and unplanned situations, such as cleaning up after a fire and removal of asbestos. It is a fast-growing enterprise, despite intensive competition, some of it from "moonlighters" working for black market contractors.

The Employee

The employee is female, born in 1966. Her education attainments are to MAVO (lower general secondary education). Her employment history includes jobs in catering, museum attendant, sales assistant, assistant manager of a petrol station, technical service assistant and finally, clerical work for a large consultancy. Her disability/medical history began with luxation of the joints from 1983 onwards. In 1990 she had an operation on a benign tumour in a knee, after which she had to learn to walk again. Her rehabilitation took around 3 months. After being ill for one year she was put on a full WAO incapacity for work benefit because of back problems and continuing problems with the knee; operated on again in 1992. She now has irreversible knee damage and malformation of pelvis and shoulder ribs The latter causes respiratory problems and severe headaches. She cannot stand for long, walk, lift, bend or hold her hands above her head. She receives an hour of physiotherapy three times per week. At the end of 1993 the Ziekenfonds (Dutch national health service) ruled that the cost of this would no longer be reimbursed from 1994. She then sought employment again.

During a reassessment for benefit at the end of 1993, she received a partial incapacity assessment but aimed to get off WAO benefit all together. She registered with temporary employment agencies, but came to the conclusion that it is very difficult to get back into employment after a period on a disability benefit. After three months, she found temporary work. While working she was called to an interview with the GAK mediating agency. She had no faith in GAK and did not feel able to take a day off work. Despite this, the GAK mediator telephoned her about a permanent job as clerical assistant in a wages administration department.

The employee joined the company in September 1994, on a permanent contract without a trial period. Problems arose initially between her and the other office staff who refused to co-operate with her. After six weeks the wage clerk sacked her without authority. The employee reported sick for four months until director reversed her dismissal and she returned to work. The wage clerk was eventually dismissed. Today, the company is managed by the director, his son and this employee as administrative assistant.

The employee places minimal emphasis on her physical disabilities. While GAK (central administration office) had imposed conditions on the physical burdens she could undertake, she disregards these. Nor have there been adjustments to her working hours. Her workplace is on the first floor and there is no lift. She has her own transport. Although she hides it, she does sometimes suffer from her condition. Since treatment to raise her pain threshold, she is not always aware of pain. Meanwhile, exostosis has developed in her other knee. She is putting off an operation as it means rehabilitation and learning to walk all over again.

Recruitment

The director was looking for someone who could grow with the company. Through GAK-Detapool he had a choice of three women. One had very poor hearing, which was unsuitable and a second postponed her interview because of a cold. The third candidate was prepared to do overtime and asked straight away when she could start. Because of this, the director did not ask what her disability was. The director had a positive attitude towards applicants with disabilities who showed strong motivation. The match between this and the candidate with an appetite for hard work and determination to find a job, proved to be good.

GAK conventionally develops a clear picture of the employees needs, abilities and weaknesses before offering placements. They then carry the employment risks, acting as employer and seconding the employee. Secondment contracts are for between six months and four years, in connection with subsidy regulations. Here, the employer preferred to offer a permanent contract straight away.

The director has been successful in recruiting energetic and hard-working people. Applicants appear of their own accord through word of mouth. Written advertising is not used. At the moment he has a pool of 150 stand-by workers available. The company takes on many people who have limited access to the labour market. One example is the employment of foreign workers. While the director requires that they can speak a little Dutch, he has taught six himself. He also recruits unemployed youths "off the football pitch" through a football club he sponsors. In principle, people with a history of involvement with drugs (if it is not too serious) will also be employed.

The director receives a subsidy from the Industrial Insurance Board for employing people with a partial capacity for work. However, he fills in the forms very briefly, through lack of time, and "if they don't like it, they can keep it". He says that he never has any problems with the authorities issuing the subsidies.

Case Study Netherlands 3: Rehabilitation Institution
Interviews were held with the employee, a former employer and the personnel officer at the current place of employment.

The Enterprise

The enterprise is a national healthcare foundation for project-based work rehabilitation for people with a background of psycho-social problems. It seeks no subsidy from the mental health authorities. Some projects are financially autonomous, others are financed by funds or from benefit agencies' payments. The aim is 'innovative improvement of care from the perspective of the user', getting clients back into work through the creation of projects. Project workers take care of some project administration themselves, part is subcontracted to a bureau which started out as a rehabilitation project.

The Employee

The employee was born in 1958. He has completed LTS (elementary technical education), evening classes for HAVO (higher general secondary education) with no diploma, various vocational courses on car and motorbike maintenance, a psychiatry course, and is presently studying psychology (third year). For 15-16 years he was a motorbike mechanic. Around the age of 30, he came to a turning point when technical work no longer satisfied him and he took interest in social studies. In 1990 he began studying psychology through the Open University, 20 hours of study per week in addition to 32 hours as a mechanic. He passed his first year examinations and signed on at the University of Utrecht.

In late 1992 he became ill with stress, exhaustion and severe headaches. During his first year of sickness he twice returned to his old work as occupational therapy. This was not a success. In late 1993 he was assessed as 100% incapacitated, through nervous exhaustion. He found some work himself as manager of a band which increased his self-confidence. In 1994, he was assessed by the GAK (central administration office) as able to work, and was put forward as a candidate He felt that mediation was very late starting and could have begun in the first year of his illness. In early 1995, he began as a project worker for the foundation with a trial period of two months. His tasks included literature study, contacts with institutions, writing up interviews and a project report. At the end of 1995 he entered employment in a sheltered living project as counsellor/supervisor (social psychiatry) for ex-psychiatric patients learning to live independently. He is taking a practice-oriented 4-month course on psychiatry.

Recruitment

To the foundation, all that is required of candidates is that they have some first-hand experience, that they want to work, and what they want to do fits in with the work the foundation has to offer. For paid work there is an application procedure. Applicants do not necessarily have to match a job profile perfectly. The director stated that people who have mental illnesses feel vulnerable and are often not strong enough to take new steps such as applying for a job. Many are unsure of their skill or interest areas, which emerge after reassessment through, for example, voluntary work. This form of rehabilitation was regarded as essential but, in practice, too few opportunities are available.

Work at the foundation was totally different to what the employee was used to. He was coached by the director once a week, a special support committee was set up through the foundation, composed of five people with special expertise. He worked 16 hours a week over four working days, he had been strictly advised by the Industrial Insurance Board not to work full days. The scope for flexibility in his work and working hours was very important. If time was short, part of his work was taken by a member of the project's support committee. He was able to clarify his preferences for work area and activity. He believed that it would be a good idea to limit the duration of work with the foundation as, in his view, working there too long would make it difficult to switch to an ordinary job.

Current Employer

The present employer is a healthcare institution with 120 employees, focusing on care for people with learning disabilities, social psychiatry, sheltered living and day centres. The general position is that clients with psychological problems can, in principle, be supported by employees who have themselves experienced such problems. In practice, this is applied on an ad hoc basis. When such an employee is recruited, a reintegration plan is drawn up and the personnel officer seeks to establish the extent to which the candidate has come to terms with his illness. In his opinion, no method is 100% watertight. For reasons of privacy, the employee did not wish to speak about his present work.

Spain

Profile of Spanish Case Studies

Business Characteristics

Case Studies	Spain 1	Spain 2	Spain 3
Trading activity	Cultural services	Sports goods manufacture	Confectionery manufacture
Established	1990	not established	late 1970s
Location	urban: Barcelona, Catalonia	urban: Barcelona, Catalonia	Guadalajara, Castilla-La Mancha
Number and gender of employees	300 total	100	10
Quota Scheme	Applicable	Applicable	Not applicable

Characteristics of Employees with Disabilities

Case Studies	Spain 1	Spain 2	Spain 3
Number of employees	2 total; 1 studied	3 total; 1 studied	1
Gender	male	male	male
Age	22	31	27
Type(s) of disability	Learning disability (Down's Syndrome)	Hearing loss and speech impairment	Slight learning disability
Education attainments	basic first level	primary and vocational education	Special school; vocational education
Job title/role	general assistant	workshop technician	production worker
Employment status	permanent	temporary	temporary
Mediating organisation (see also Glossary)	Proyecto Aura	Municipal Labour Assessment and Integration Team (EAL)	Self-help association (Asociación Las Encinas)

Case Study Spain 1: Cultural Services

Interviews were held with the employee, the workplace mentor and the mediating organisation's psychologist.

The enterprise

The enterprise manages a broad range of museums and cultural centres, as well as the promotion of cultural, recreational and related research activities.

The Employee

The employee, aged 22 and with a mild learning disability, was placed in the enterprise in 1994 on a temporary contract as an office assistant. After three years, following a positive assessment of his performance, he was given a permanent contract. He left school at 16, completing the normal course of basic general education and then spent three years preparing for employment at the Aura Project, where he attended classes, meetings and leisure activities with other people sharing his disability. Aged 19, he was put forward as a suitable candidate for an advertised vacancy.

He is one of two employees with learning disabilities and they alternate between two different jobs on a weekly basis, (photocopying and a documentation centre). The employer found that the staff preferred to change jobs regularly, even when the tasks carried out were simple and repetitive. Two ways in which the employee had to develop in order to integrate were identified: acceptance of the hierarchical company structure and mixing with work colleagues. The relationship between the two employees is difficult so the employer avoids having them do the same activity together for long. Their relationships with other employees are good, although there can sometimes be communications problems and they can create delays. Work efficiency is slightly less than that of other employees, but there are great differences between the two: in the case chosen for this study, performance is 90% and work is finished to a high standard. The other employee is less efficient and has poorer attendance. The case study employee feels very comfortable in the enterprise and plays a large part in the social activities organised by staff.

Recruitment

When vacancies arose, job specifications were determined. Three methods are used to source applicants: advertisements in the media, looking through CVs submitted, and, in some cases, the use of employment agencies. Candidates with some form of disability were given priority over other applicants because of the statutory 2% quota but they must match the required profile The quota was recognised because the enterprise is a "charity" and must demonstrate "awareness".

To recruit people with a disability the enterprise relied on mediation organisations such as the Aura Project. The employer believed that their professional mediation was essential for people with learning disabilities, in facilitating both access to employment and integration at work during the first weeks or months. While this function could be performed by the National Employment Institute (INEM), a state body, it was unable to provide personal assistance. The Aura Project ensured that there would be no additional cost to the company. A job coach initially accompanied a new employee to work every day (in this case for two months) and the company's personnel officers completed a regular questionnaire. The job coach support tapered off as employment progressed, though the monitoring questionnaire continued for a time afterwards.

The enterprise chose a female employee to act as a mentor and take over the function of the job coach. In her view, she is an important interface between the employee with a disability and other employees. The mentor believed that people with learning disabilities could not be integrated into a firm in the same way as other staff. In her opinion, recruitment policies should not be governed exclusively by the logic of profit and competitiveness.

In contrast, the personnel manager believed that employees with a disability should do work suited to their potential under the same conditions as other staff, viewing financial incentives as inferior treatment or discrimination. However, social awareness was considered important. Lack of awareness was thought to be due to a mixture of prejudices (which cease when the people affected are known personally) and happy ignorance.

Case Study Spain 2: Sports Products Manufacture

Interviews were held with the manager's assistant, the section head and the mediating organisation's social worker. No interview was conducted with the worker himself owing to his specific problems in communicating.

The Enterprise

This enterprise is part of a French multinational, specialising in sports products. The ownership structure did not become apparent until the interview. In Spain, the enterprise has various production units and 15 large shops handling sales and repairs. The Barcelona centre, at which the case study was conducted, has an average of 100 employees. Below management level, most staff are sales personnel and workshop technicians. The majority are students, aged between 20 and 22 on average, who work 20 hours per week, hired on a temporary basis for a few months. Their incomes are low (Ptas 40,000 per month) but there is great demand for the jobs. The company has its own training scheme for employees, currently solely in France. The major trade unions are not represented but a works council represents the staff and employees are encouraged to participate in company affairs, facilitated by a monthly meeting in each section. In view of the low average age of employees, there is a friendly working atmosphere. Most of the employees see their work as temporary.

The Employee

There are currently two employees with disabilities, in both cases with hearing and speech impairments. The employer is currently proposing to hire several other workers with physical disabilities, as they have identified suitable work and they wish to achieve the 2% quota target. The case study involves a man aged 31, who received primary education at a special centre for deaf children, obtaining the basic school certificate. He then undertook vocational training for two years before working as an apprentice in a carpentry workshop then as a builder's assistant for four years. Finally, he was taken on for six months at a Special Employment Centre, a sheltered scheme, which assembles cables for SEAT cars.

He obtained the job less than a year ago within the framework of a work experience course organised by the EAL agency. This course consisted of 100 hours in a classroom and 200 hours of work experience which took place within this enterprise without payment. The experience led to the company hiring him on a temporary contract for 20 hours per week, on similar terms to the other workers.

In view of his hearing and speech impairment, his job does not involve meeting the public. Communication with colleagues and managers was and remains a problem, he can only partially understand spoken language. In addition to his disability, the employee was shy and lacking in confidence. He is very responsible in his tasks and he carries them out well although he has difficulty adapting himself flexibly to changes, in which case communication problems constitute a substantial barrier. This barrier also prevents him from exploiting the employee participation channels available at the enterprise. The problem is exacerbated by his low academic qualifications, as these limit his writing and reading ability. He requires more training and supervision than other workers. However, his responsibility and receptive attitude mean that the enterprise considers him to be an acceptable employee.

In view of the age of the worker and his wish to settle down, his expectations are very different from those of most of his colleagues. His employer is aware of this and is considering giving him a new contract with longer hours but this is limited by the availability of work for which he is capable.

Recruitment

For the few staff with a high level of responsibility, advertisements are placed in the press. The majority of employees, however, are recruited by shop window advertisement and word of mouth among students. Section heads are responsible for selecting their team, with management approval. Candidates are normally expected to have prior knowledge of the product they are going to sell.

In 1996, the enterprise decided to meet the quota 2% target due to the personal, but unspecified, "awareness" of the shopping centre manager. The enterprise sought out three mediating organisations to achieve this. In the case of EAL, an agreement was made to offer three people work experience. A job coach provided them with support to learn the job, tapering off as company supervisors and work colleagues took over to facilitate integration. Evaluation by EAL continued with regular visits to the agency office and telephone contact between the section head and the EAL monitoring officer. One of the three placements did not develop due to poor attendance.

Case Study Spain 3: Confectionery Manufacturer

Interviews were held with the employee, employer and the mediating organisation's placement officer and trainer.

The Enterprise

This traditional confectionery patisserie manufacturer is a small family business located in a provincial capital close to Madrid. The products are hand-produced. The enterprise's market is declining as major food businesses from Madrid and elsewhere increase their market share.

The Employee

There have been two people with disabilities employed in this enterprise. The previous person, known to the owner's family, worked for six months and had adjusted well, but he found a job with better hours. The employee did not take up tax incentives and subsidies owing to ignorance and the short time he was employed. The current employee is 27 and has slight learning disabilities. He was trained at vocational centres and special schools until completing the basic cycle, with some delay. He spent several years in a Special Employment Centre linked to Asociación Las Encinas, an association of families and professionals dealing with people with disabilities. He was trained in various manual services, during which he received a professional qualification in handling food. Two months ago, he was put forward as a candidate at the request of the confectionery company. His mediators had been investigating possible recruitment opportunities.

The employee is still in the practical experience phase and under the supervision of the trainer. Work performance, in the employer's opinion, is low in terms of ability to clearly understand tasks, but the his motivation and willingness make up for this. Productivity is within the usual margins at his level. He has difficulty in remembering work instructions which is being resolved using writing instructions kept in front of him. Although he had poor self-esteem initially, he is happy with his work and keen to progress. The trainer believes that he is settling in well and now requires virtually no supervision.

The employer feels that integration has been smooth and stresses the initiative shown in areas with which he was already familiar. His employment required no change in the pace of work. The employer felt that family businesses might be more willing to take on such people than large companies, in which the production line allows no time for contemplation. He finds qualifications less important than trust and an interest in the job. There has been no openly negative reaction from work colleagues who, partly also because of the age difference, treat him with a degree of paternal condescension.

Recruitment

Staffing in this enterprise has been quite stable. On the one hand, the majority of employees have been moving towards retirement in the company or have been there for some years and, on the other hand, the participation of members of the family at peak times is normal. The work was considered unattractive for young people due to unsociable hours, lack of automation and the decline of the sector.

For the mediators, the willingness of the employer to hire the employee stands out, although it was not the first contact between them. Students from the vocational centre were already working for other enterprises run by members of the employer's family. The employer openly identified as the prime reason the benefit of reduced social security contributions with a job subsidy if the contract becomes permanent.

The employee is comfortable in his current work but he would prefer another activity in which he could develop broader personal relationships. He is currently taking driving lessons in order to be able to work as a delivery man (either for this business or another company). The employer recognises that he will leave if he finds something better and appears phlegmatic about this: it is a fall-back and, possibly, transient employment sector even for the person with a disability.

United Kingdom

Profile of British Case Studies

This section presents the case material which forms the basis of the UK analysis. Problems encountered in recruitment cases meant that three case studies as specified were not achieved. The material that was collected, however, provides a rich source of information.

Case Study UK 1: The Cleaning Agency

Interviews were held with the employee, the owner-manager of the enterprise and the mediating organisation.

The Enterprise

This business undertook contracts for general office and domestic cleaning. Most contracts were small, typically on site in small offices. Most cleaning staff were women working part-time. There were 4 supervisors, and 2 full-time specialist cleaning services cleaners. Pay rates were low with no holiday or sick pay. Many employees had earnings below employee and employer liabilities for National Insurance (social welfare) contributions.

Business Characteristics

Case Studies	UK 1	UK 2	UK 3	UK 4	UK 5	UK 6
Trading activity	Cleaning agency	Textile factory	Nursing home	Manu-facturing	Con-struction	Manu-facturing
Established	c. 1981	c. 1976				
Location	urban: conurbation	urban: inner city	urban: city suburb	urban: conurbation	urban: conurbation	urban: conurbation
Number of employees	120	16	35	c. 20	50	50
Disability Discrimina-tion Act	Applicable	Not applicable	Applicable	Applicable	Applicable	Applicable

Characteristics of Employees with Disabilities

Case Studies	UK 1	UK 2	UK 3	UK 4	UK 5	UK 6
Number of employees	1	model cases	model cases	1	1	1
Gender	female			male	male	male
Age	early 40s			22	mid 30s	50s
Type(s) of disability	mental illness			mild learning disability	Muscular Dystrophy	epilepsy, slight hearing loss
Job title/role	office cleaner			factory operative	data input	general assistant
Employment status	part time			full time, 50% subsidy	full time, majority subsidy	full time
Mediator (see also Glossary)	JobReach			JobAhead	JobReach	JobReach

The Employee

The employee reported a long period in hospital during 1995-96 with severe clinical depression, which has occasionally recurred since her first spell of illness as a young woman. A hospital social worker introduced her to JobReach, who then approached the enterprise. A supervisor from the enterprise visited her and took her to an office that needed a cleaner. She accepted this job straight away. She had not enjoyed this first job as she had lost confidence, and did not find the clients friendly. Her supervisor realised she was not happy and, when another vacancy came up, offered her a change of office where she has remained.

The employee was currently working from 4.00pm to 5.30pm five days weekly. She was still suffering symptoms of depression but found the work ideal in helping her towards recovery and she had not had to take time off sick. Eventually, she hoped to work longer hours, in a slightly more demanding job. She had previously worked in jobs where she had more responsibility. Presently she did not feel ready to move on and found it best to take a fairly short time perspective: looking too far ahead provoked anxieties that became overwhelming.

Recruitment

Recruitment for general cleaning work was often handled directly by supervisors. There was no formal recruitment policy, and the employee did not receive a written contract. Employees had to be reliable and trustworthy, able to maintain relationships with office staff, and work around client's activities. The enterprise depended on the local availability of people prepared to move between premises as needed to meet clients' requirements. The client base constantly changed and there was rapid staff turnover. The employer looked for 'good fits' between client requirements and cleaners to keep reliable staff and cleaning contracts. This could be an advantage to people whose first job did not work well: it was worth the employer's while to find a different 'slot', rather than ask the employee to leave.

The employer had recruited a woman with a partial hearing loss through JobReach. Problems arose as she was not able to communicate well with the clients and she was moved to a different office where the clients did not expect to talk to her so much. The owner had not heard of any further problems. Mental health problems, though harder to manage, would be approached the same way. Access problems would make the employment of a wheelchair user unlikely.

The support offered by the mediator was of key importance to the employee who felt unable alone to take the initiative needed to get a job at that stage in her recovery. For the employer, the mediator functioned as a free recruitment agency, sharing some of the selection work as long as their choices were reliable.

Support Measures

The mediator had found that clients with mental health problems face special problems if they have a condition where their ability to work fluctuates. She commented that schemes such as the Supported Placement Scheme were rarely used as it could be hard to assess the rate at which wages should be subsidised within the formal requirements of the programme.

Case Study UK 2: The textile factory

An interview was held with the employer. Model cases were used as no employees wished to participate in the research.

The Enterprise

The factory made domestic textile furnishings. The business operated from the two floors of a large Victorian industrial building, in an inner city area. The premises were rented and cheap, but poorly accessible and run-down. Heating was a problem and staff frequently worked in outdoor clothes and hats. Work was also taken to two outworkers who worked at home on a self-employed basis, a traditional form of employment in the local textile industry. Wages were generally low, comprising an hourly rate, a personal productivity bonus and an attendance bonus. Seasonal fluctuations meant that the factory experienced a Christmas 'rush', starting in October. The first months of the year were slackest. The employer had some previous professional experience as an auxiliary nurse.

Recruitment

The owner was responsible for recruitment and selection. There was no formal procedure. Word-of-mouth applicants often proved satisfactory. They knew from their friend or relative what the work involved, and had already thought about their suitability. Personal friendships helped keep the workforce together. The business relied on staff flexibility and loyalty to deal with fluctuations in trade. Solidarity among workers was considered important, to co-operate to fulfil orders in rush times and share out unpopular work. The friendly atmosphere and relative informality of the factory was thought important to encourage staff to stay and acted as partial compensation for the discomfort of the building, and low wages.

Applicants were invited to try out the work, something expected among skilled workers in the trade, employers and the workforce. It provided an opportunity for staff to see the potential recruit and their views were sought. Health or any disability issues were not raised by the employer. The owner tried to retain staff and give second chances to people with poor attendance or low work standards. These presented a problem to other workers who had to adapt their work schedules to accommodate outstanding tasks affecting the bonus scheme. The owner "had to balance compassion with sound business management".

Employees with Disabilities

The owner had one employee considered disabled by a long-standing condition, but preferred not to discuss that employee's circumstances. A person with a disability with lower productivity would be unlikely to be approved by the workforce, who stood to lose financially if they had to help somebody with lower productivity, due to the pay structure. The employer would be heavily influenced by their assessment. Despite this, familial or friendship connections were valuable and could make a difference. Poor access, heating and working conditions meant that it would be hard for some people with disabilities to work in this environment. The employer was prepared to consider possibilities of improving access or the environment for candidates who had ideal skills and experience, but she was sceptical that it would be easy or relatively inexpensive to achieve this. She had little knowledge or understanding about schemes which could assist.

Case Study UK 3: The nursing home

An interview was held with the employer using model cases. Employees with disabilities were not interviewed.

The Enterprise

The nursing home offered long-term nursing care and short-stay or respite care. The patients were mostly elderly people, with a small number of much younger patients, all dependent on nursing care for maintenance of life. Wage rates depended on qualifications and job descriptions.

Employees with Disabilities

One employee, the kitchen assistant, had learning disabilities and was paid a small wage of £15, up to the limit of the income support earnings disregard. The employer believed that people with this disability could often be relied upon to reach higher standards in some tasks than non-disabled people who got bored more easily. She had found that they were often meticulous in finishing tasks, and not distracted or waylaid. The manager currently employed two members of staff whose work capacity and productivity was lowered through age or ill-health on compassionate grounds. One employee had passed retirement age and was now less energetic and capable than previously, but was retained through loyalty. A second staff member was awaiting surgery and no longer able to work as a care assistant, she was offered a few hours domestic work when she was able to come to work.

Access to the nursing home office was difficult for wheelchair users as it had a narrow door. The manager was unaware of the availability of financial support to make the office accessible. She was uncertain about employing someone with epilepsy in some roles, in view of the risk of an accident. She would expect to discuss such a case with her insurance broker. Age and/or hearing loss would be no disadvantage. Older workers were preferred, as more mature, more likely to stay and better able to get on well with each other.

Recruitment

There was no written recruitment policy. Vacancies for trained nurses were hard to fill, but only rarely arose. The less qualified workforce was more mobile. The manager tried to recruit local people, as this made it easier to manage shifts and rotas. Health and disability issues were not specifically raised in job interviews but work requirements were stressed. The manager described herself as ready to give people a chance, becoming less judgmental during her experience running a nursing home. Asked about the reactions of residents or visitors, she thought that the recruitment of a person with a disability would reflect positively on the enterprise, as a caring and competent place.

The kitchen assistant was appointed when a new member of staff, who had supervised her in her previous job, explained that he was leaving and asked the new manager if there was another vacancy. The manager had received several promotional mailshots from JobAhead previously but had discarded them, believing that people referred would not achieve the standard of work required. Now, however, she got in touch with the mediator and the person was offered a job, initially part-time. The employee had now been in the post for 12 months and worked well with no problems. The manager later took on a care assistant with a learning disability through JobAhead, but that appointment was not successful. His attendance was poor and he was eventually asked to leave.

Case Studies UK 4, 5 and 6

Three employees agreed to participate in this study but their employers declined the invitation. The following case studies therefore comprise a set of interviews with employees and support workers. To some extent, the circumstances of these employees match those presented in the model cases discussed with participating employers, and further light is thrown on issues that were identified by those employers as important.

Case Study UK 4: The Factory Worker

This employee was 22 years old with mild learning disabilities. He found it hard to maintain conversation for long; his parents helped him to manage the discussion. He worked for a small manufacturing firm as a production worker. He worked 35 hours each week for a net weekly wage of £115. He agreed with his parents that he liked going to work. He also liked the additional income. He had previously had a benefit income during attendance at a training centre. His parents also appreciated the contribution he was able to make to household income. The worker from JobAhead, considered that this was a very successful example of a Supported Placement. The employer had approached JobAhead themselves, in response to promotional material mailed to small firms in the area. The employee with a disability had learned quickly how to do the work required, working alongside a job trainer for the first two weeks. Direct support had then been withdrawn, although contact had been maintained. His wages were subsidised by 50% under Supported Placement arrangements. The employee had had an accident at work, although he and his parents made light of this. He had burnt his hand during the work process, and had needed hospital treatment.

Case Study UK 5: The Computer Operator

This employee had muscular dystrophy and now had limited mobility and some problems with speech. He tired easily and needed to be extra warm. His wife cared for him at home, with domiciliary help from the local authority. She took her husband to work by car, and drove him home every day. The employee currently worked for a local building firm for 35 hours each week, inputting data from order forms onto the firm's computer. He worked alongside the manager in a small office and was paid a net wage of £133. More than half was subsidised under a support scheme. The employee claimed Disability Working Allowance to top up this low wage, and help meet household expenses.

He had been in this job for several years, sourced through JobReach. Since then his condition had deteriorated and problems have arisen in respect of the equipment and workplace adaptations needed to maintain his capacity to work. He and the mediator described delays and difficulties in negotiating the purchase of a powered wheelchair when he needed this to continue to work. The mediator believed that the employee had almost lost his job as a result. There were further problems concerning the construction of an office access ramp involving misunderstandings about whether or not the work would be covered by the 'Access to Work' financial support scheme for workplace adaptations. The employee was uncomfortable about this misunderstanding.

Both the employee and his partner recognised the inevitable deterioration associated with his disability. He hoped to keep his job as long as possible.

Although he expressed anxiety about his productivity, the mediator saw him as a steady and methodical worker, a considerable resource to his employers.

Case Study UK 6: The General Assistant

This employee worked as a cleaner and general assistant for a design and manufacturing company. He worked 37 hours weekly, and earned £511 gross monthly. He had been unemployed for several years before taking this job, assisted by JobReach. He had a slight hearing loss and suffered from epilepsy, controlled with medication. Throughout his life he had undertaken a number of unskilled, low paid jobs, interspersed with periods of unemployment. Medication for epilepsy had improved as he got older, but what might appear now as a relatively mild disability had had a profound effect on his working life.

The employee had also had an accident at work. He made light of this himself, but the accident had required attendance at hospital and a period off work. It is not known whether or not the accident was directly connected with his hearing loss. The employer did not respond to requests for interview and, shortly after the interview with the employee, the researcher learned that the firm had ceased trading at short notice.

Chapter 5   Consolidating the Case Studies

Introduction

This chapter presents an analysis of the case studies in six Member States, drawing heavily on case study and other materials from national research reports. In analysing the case studies, it must be recognised that the majority have been sourced through mediating organisations specialising in placing people with disabilities in employment. The extent to which the cases reflect the overall picture of people with disabilities in employment in SMEs is not possible to ascertain easily. Alternative methods of sourcing cases were unsuccessfully made by research teams in each Member State participating in the study, which demonstrated that the possible sample size in each state was very small and inferred that there is a strong case for the approach adopted.

The analysis is presented in four sections, each considering the impact on the employment of people with disabilities in small and medium sized enterprises and presenting barriers to employment together with good practice:

The Legislative Framework

- Incentives for employment, including financial incentives for employees; financial incentives for employers; aids and adaptations;

- Compulsory measures and obligations promoting employment or retention, including: anti-discrimination legislation; employment quotas; protection against dismissal;

- Related employment policy, including: Health and Safety legislation; Sickness and Health legislation.

Employee Characteristics

- The nature and severity of the disability;

- Employees' age; gender and educational attainment;

- Confidence and self-esteem;

- Employee integration and development.

Employer and Workplace-Related Characteristics

- Workplace organisation and decision making;

- Recruitment practices;

- Attitudes towards disability, including perceptions of risk and social awareness;

- Enterprise trade sector

- Employment terms and conditions;

- Employee representation;

- Workspace accessibility.

Mediating Organisations

- Matching candidates to needs;

- Information provision;

- Reducing risk;

- On the job support;

- Promoting confidence and self-esteem;

- Differentiating between mediating organisations.

The Legislative Framework

The Legislative Framework:

- Incentives for employment, including financial incentives for employees; financial incentives for employers; aids and adaptations;

- Compulsory measures and obligations promoting employment or retention, including: anti-discrimination legislation; employment quotas; protection against dismissal;

- Related employment policy, including: Health and Safety legislation; Sickness and Health legislation.

Introduction

Legislation promoting the employment of people with disabilities in European Union Member States has been characterised by Lunt and Thornton (1993), among others, as tending towards compulsory employment measures while countries such as Canada, Australia and the United States have focused more on anti-discrimination and equal opportunities legislation.

As stated in chapter 3, while a considerable blurring of these boundaries has occurred over recent years, a line can still be drawn between countries positioning legislation on disability within the context of a broad anti-discrimination policy and those operating compartmentalised measures such as quota schemes (Thornton and Lunt, 1997).

This broad characterisation is limited both in the impact of public policy on small and medium sized enterprises, which are often excluded from statutory obligations due to their size, and in terms of the spectrum of policies and applicability that exists at Member State level.

However, despite these differences, while each Member State operates a range of voluntary and compulsory measures, and while some focus primarily on particular types of promotion or obligation, the actual impact and consequences of these policies at employer and employee level appears broadly similar.

Financial Incentives for Employees

In both Britain and Ireland, differences between the forms and levels of financial support available to economically inactive and employed people with disabilities were identified as fundamental barriers to taking employment. This issue did not arise in other Member States studies.

While the British national research team found a strong preference for work over unemployment in their study, taking up work opportunities depends on the feasibility of the complete financial income package people with disabilities are able to put together. The impact of work on overall household earnings and state benefits income makes a critical difference.

People with disabilities are entitled, in both countries, to claim means tested income support benefits. These regulations can permit payment for work up to a set limit for those in receipt of general income-related benefits. People with disabilities in receipt of benefits relating to disability or incapacity for work can also receive payment for 'therapeutic' work up to an earnings limit and for a certain therapeutic period before losing their entitlement.

The British team noted that, for those people who are (or whose partner is) in receipt of means tested benefits, only very part-time work might be feasible. While this situation might suit some people's needs temporarily, because of financial pressures on the household or as a route into the world of work, employment rights and access to holiday or sick pay may be limited in part time work.

The risks attached to loss of state benefits on commencement of employment are substantial. In Ireland, the research team calculated that people with a disability who are economically inactive receive a Disability Allowance worth £64.50 per week in 1996/97, and are allowed to earn an additional £35.20 per week. With additional free bus travel and medical facilities, the total package was estimated at £120 per week. As a result of this and employment taxes, for a person to come off benefit they would have to earn over £150 per week simply to maintain their standard of living:

> "People with a learning disability will typically have no second level qualifications and therefore will enter the job market at the lowest entry point of £110 or £120 per week. Enterprise 2 said that if he were to pay a full wage of £200 he would need to get a full output of work from the employee, which may not be possible." (Irish national report).

Most employees in Ireland aspired to giving up their benefits in favour of a full salary in the company they worked for. A lack of information amongst those employees about their entitlements was, however, striking. It was unclear to them whether or not, or how, they could ever return to their previous benefits if they lost their job for any reason. Employment opportunities for people with disabilities are limited due to a range of factors presented later in this chapter. Such limitations – such as dependency on high levels of supervision or the necessity for specialised and long term training programmes – might not be taken into account by state benefits assessors convinced of a person's employment track record. An Irish mediating organisation stated that there can be lengthy delays in securing benefits if a person loses their job, delays which could cause personal hardship.

In Britain, a Disability Working Allowance (DWA), provides on-going support to people in employment and is designed to top-up the income of those with low earnings. There was, however, no evidence from the research that the benefit acts as an incentive to employers. Beneficiaries of a supported placement scheme were unsure about how this contributed to their wages.

Most of the employees interviewed for the Irish case studies retained medical cards entitling them to free health care during their first year of a supported employment scheme. Medical cards are available to all people who are economically inactive. The employee in case study Ireland 3, at the end of his first year in work, was about to lose his medical card. The high medical costs associated with maintaining control over his mental illness meant that he was to go onto a drugs subsidisation scheme. While this will cover some of the cost of his drugs, the first £30 per month, £360 per year, is excluded. In addition, schizophrenia is a condition which commonly leads to the experience of more health problems – including digestive problems, influenza, bronchitis – and thus a greater need for medical support.

Financial Incentives for Employers

"From the point of view of the enterprise taking on the worker, a combination of motives was involved: firstly, *the suitability of the candidate for the job* as an "assistant" and, secondly, the lower economic cost of hiring the worker owing to his handicap" (Spanish national study).

While awareness of financial incentives for the employment of people with disabilities appeared to be low, particularly in countries without enforced employment quota systems, the use of mediating organisations by employers in these case studies helped to mitigate the problem in case study enterprises. Commonly, mediators take on a dual information provision role – informing employers of schemes for which potential employees might be eligible – and facilitation role – assisting employers to successfully utilise those programmes.

Types of support available include:

* support for interviews;
* premiums for the employment of a person with a disability;
* wage subsidies; and
* exemptions from social insurance or other statutory charges;
* workplace aids and adaptations.

Support for Interviews

Support for interviews was referred to only in the Irish study. In this case, the availability of information about the support available appeared to be the key problem:

"Although the NRB does provide a grant for the use of an interpreter [for people with hearing impairments] in interviews, companies do not appear to know about these or other grants which they could avail of." (Irish national report).

Despite the concern about dissemination, employers focus primarily on the employment advantages and disadvantages of the employment of a person with a disability, and the costs likely to arise in the longer term, rather than short term or recruitment-oriented measures, as will be shown below.

Employment Premiums

Lump sum employment premiums were referred to in two national studies. In Spain, the premium payment provided the only example of a company seeking to employ someone primarily because of the financial support available. Economic incentives in Spain include an exemption from a substantial share of social insurance contributions and a large (one million pesetas) premium payment on the signing of an open-ended employment contract. The advantage of the premium was not a determining factor in two of the Spanish cases, but: "acquire much greater relevance in case no. 3, a small enterprise in a sector in crisis which is in great need of capital." (Spanish national report). The value of the premium was questioned by one employer:

> "the manager in case no. 2 considers that this is discrimination which "degrades" the worker." (Spanish national report).

In France, their appropriateness was also questioned by an employer and the researcher:

> "The current system for allocating these premiums does not actually provide any means of limiting the risk of "bounty-hunting", where the employer has no intention of keeping the disabled person whose recruitment earned the premium. In such a case the employer would look for the next opportunity for easy profit, thereby creating scope for unfair competition based on certain employers' lack of scruples... More generally, this windfall does not sway the recruitment decision, because that decision affects the viability of the enterprise over a longer period than a single payment; unless he has particular financial requirements, the employer will pocket a premium which cannot play a part in his decision-making. That is what is called a windfall effect..." (French national report).

Three further difficulties were noted:

- it is resented by employers who criticise the 'windfall effect' "because it normally contributes to a heavier burden in taxes and social security contributions without giving the enterprise any long-term return." To some extent, and perhaps because of the 'bounty hunting' referred to above, employers "regard it as an unwarranted advantage and feel guilty about it, because it makes them appear to be using slave labour." (French national report).

- the impact on the appointed person with a disability can be negative. "The other employees might actually consider the newcomer to have been "sold" or "knocked down" to the company, which would do nothing to enhance his prospects of achieving recognition on his own merits." Similarly, the employee might feel that "his skills are inferior, because society has paid for him to be employed." (French national report).

- it is unclear to both employee and employer who is the real beneficiary. "The primary aim of the recruitment, to provide skills in exchange for a wage and vice versa, is liable to be lost from sight." (French national report).

The French researcher state that many of these aspects, particularly the second, remain out from sight. While it did appear that premiums "unlocked the door to some enterprises", such as those with start up or other financial needs, it was concluded that:

> "The French legislation under which small enterprises can be offered incentives to employ disabled persons, including recruitment premiums, play a flagship role, but perhaps the real key role is played by the system for the placement and support of disabled jobseekers..." (French national report).

Wages Subsidies

Wages subsidies were the most common form of financial support available. The most commonly stated reason for using the support available was the reduction in the resulting risk of taking on someone with a disability.

> "While the subsidy was not seen as the main reason for recruiting people with disabilities, it did make it easier for two of the enterprises to do so. Enterprise 1, which did not have to pay its employee for the first year at all, said that this removed the financial risk involved in employing someone with a disability but emphasised that it was a matter of mutual benefit... Three of the enterprises recommended that

incentives be provided to prospective employers to make up for any fall in productivity and/or higher management and supervision costs. Two of the enterprises were employing people with disabilities without receiving a subsidy but, in one case, they only topped up the DA [Disability income Allowance] ... which is effectively a wage subsidy. They both stated that the financial incentive was not really a factor in employing people with disabilities; one because they found that the people with disabilities were more highly motivated and committed than other staff, and the other because the lower financial cost was offset by higher supervision costs." (Irish national report).

Despite this, the availability of financial support was rarely the key reason for the employment of a person with a disability. The German research team stated that employers appeared to be willing to take on people with disabilities "because of the financial assistance they can obtain". Despite this, and perhaps because substantial or full funding is provided at the outset which ends entirely after a maximum of three years:

"Financial considerations are seldom the deciding factor in the recruitment of disabled workers, although they always make the decision easier. Most employers take account of the fact that the employment relationship is permanent whereas the financial assistance is only for a limited period." and: "If assistance is to be an incentive for employing disabled workers it must be at a level such that employers are prepared to accept the inherent risk that the employment relationship might fail." (German national report).

People with disabilities are not the only group that attract employment incentives. Financial assistance is also available in Germany and other Member States for the employment of non-disabled people that are long-term unemployed. The keys to the success - and the problems with the imperfections of wage subsidies - lie in the calculation and meeting of the need that is to be addressed. In Germany, employers and placement agencies engage in "frequent disputes" about the wages that are to be paid and the tapering off of financial support limits the long-term value of employing a person with clear constraints on their performance and ability to work. Nevertheless:

"...supplementary assistance paid by the employment office in addition to the regular grants for recruiting and employing disabled workers has proved particularly useful in finding jobs for "difficult cases", where without 100% assistance the workers concerned would have had no chance of obtaining jobs from employers on the primary labour market." (German national report).

Exemptions from Social Insurance or Other Statutory Charges

Such exemptions are available in both France and Spain. In the French study:

> "...employers seem to believe that exemptions from statutory charges, which are granted today in France to promote the access or return to work of people with social difficulties, are more lucrative and easier to administer." (French national study)

This is in many ways unsurprising. When contrasted with medium or longer term wage subsidies, exemptions reduce on-going implementation or compliance costs rather than increase them.

Aids and Adaptations

In Ireland, the Netherlands and the UK, awareness of the existence of publicly funded aids and adaptations schemes to support the integration of employees with a disability appeared low, and their existence consequently had little effect on the recruitment policies of the SMEs in this study. When asked, employers in these three countries stated that these schemes were not a decisive factor in their recruitment decisions.

In Ireland, while all of the enterprises studied had problems with physical accessibility to a greater or lesser extent, none of the employers involved professed to having basic information about the assistance they could call on to adapt their buildings and facilities. In the Dutch study, awareness appeared limited to enterprises offering services specifically in the healthcare field, and awareness was not always translatable into action.

The Dutch research team noted that employees with disabilities are more readily taken on if no complicated adaptations to the workplace are necessary, or if these can be provided relatively easily and at low cost.

Of particular concern was case study Netherlands 2, in the employment of a wheelchair user by a nursing home from 1982. Few workplace adaptations were required by virtue of the access needs of patients using the company's services. However, in 1994 when the employee experienced back problems and applied to the state Industrial Insurance Board for a new wheelchair the process was lengthy, time consuming and problematic. A wheelchair was provided in November 1996 but was found to be unsuitable by the employer's own rehabilitation specialist, requiring a new application. In total, the employee has twice been given an unsuitable wheelchair. As a result of the back pain and subsequent emotional problems, the employee became ill and took a state

(WAO) disability benefit, working only as occupational therapy. Not only was there a consequent loss to the state through the loss of earnings and requirement for state support, but the employer was also significantly affected.

Similarly, in the UK, the computer operator and mediating agency in case study UK 5 reported delays and difficulties in securing a powered wheelchair when this was required to continue employment. Both the employee and the mediating organisation supporting his application believed that the employee had almost lost his job as a result of these difficulties. It appeared that the process was better suited to people commencing employment than a person with a progressive disability who required additional support to retain his job.

Transport was also identified as an issue by a respondent in the Irish study, where many buses are not accessible for wheelchair users and an example was given of one employee who earned £150 net per week and who had to pay £75 per week for transport. Such employment related costs do not receive support in the Irish situation.

The British research team state that:

> "Encouragement and emotional support from others in the household were essential for disabled people unaccustomed to, or trying to re-enter, work. People with physical impairments and mental health problems needed support to get ready for work each day, as well as to get to work, and for this they were dependent on family members. Although public transport routes were relatively convenient, buses were not wheel-chair accessible and people with fluctuating mental and physical conditions could not guarantee the stamina for public transport travel. There was no apparent input from the ATW programme's Assisted Fares to Work. In some cases, unwillingness to be seen as a disabled person discouraged exploration of government programmes." (UK national report)

Difficulties also occurred in the UK 5 case study over the construction of a ramp to permit access into the employee's place of work involving misunderstandings about whether or not the expense would be met under the 'Access to Work' scheme (ATW). The employee, a person with a progressive disease, felt concerned about the implications of such misunderstandings for the future of his employment with the firm.

This scheme aims to encourage employers to recruit disabled people, through one-off payments to purchase equipment or convert premises and provision of support workers. However, the British research team note that assistance is possible only if the potential employee is defined as disabled for the purposes of the scheme and applies to a local branch of a state service:

> "The design of the programme ... assumes that applicants, or those acting on their behalf, will draw employers' attention to relevant help available from the scheme... The employers interviewed in the study were not aware of ATW. Although they had taken on disabled people supported by specialist agencies, those employees' disabilities - learning difficulties and mental illness - are not typically addressed by the practical help provided by ATW." (UK national report)

In the UK case studies, interest in the potential of the scheme was generated by the physical obstacles identified in employing a wheelchair user with attractive skills. The British team state in their national report that:

> "In one case, assistance with internal physical alterations would sway the employment decision. In a second case, where readjustment of working routines would also be needed, costly and difficult major alterations were assumed to be beyond the scope of a government-funded programme and likely to impose costs on the employer; moreover, official scrutiny of possibly sub-standard working conditions may not have been welcomed." (UK national report)

In Spain, while none of the three employers needed to make physical adaptations to their premises:

> "in their opinion, nevertheless, many employers are reluctant to hire candidates with physical disabilities because of the high costs which alterations involving building work entail (assistance available from the government is said to be limited and complicated to arrange)." (Spanish national report)

In the Netherlands 1 case, the state Social Security Executive Office specified a covered, heated parking place for the employee. She had previously been provided with an accessible parking space for her specially-adapted car, on loan from the Industrial Insurance Board. However, the local authority's building regulations would not have permitted such a structure to be built. The problem was, in the end, solved by the purchase of a different type of transport. The Dutch research team note that:

> "applications for permission to adapt the workplace are quite often turned down by official bodies. For example, the labour inspectorate

will not approve stair lifts if other employees run the risk of being injured by them." (Dutch national report)

Such contradictions in public policy do not effectively meet stated employment aims for people with disabilities. These delays are time consuming for employee and employer. Potentially, this could adversely affect the future willingness or ability of the employer to enter into the risk perceived in employing people with disabilities.

In contrast to the perceived bureaucracy and financial limitations of these schemes, in Germany - where an employment quota scheme is enforced - workplace modification grants are sometimes seen positively as modernisation grants by providers. Local welfare offices:

> "point out that some firms use the grants they provide for workplace design and equipment as a sort of investment aid, or even specifically apply for them for modernisation work. However, this is not regarded as a problem if there are jobs for the disabled involved. In fact, employers are sometimes offered funding for workplace design and equipment by the welfare office in the form of a modernisation grant which, taken together with the assistance paid for employing a disabled worker, means that the firm always gets a "good deal"." (German national report).

Anti-Discrimination Legislation

Conceptually, anti-discrimination legislation views disability as a social issue rather than a medical one. It takes the position that many of the barriers that people with a disability face arise out of medical and charitable models of disability, and the consequent lack of integration, invisibility, and abnormality.

Although the fieldwork for the British study took place in the months around the implementation of the employment provisions contained in the country's new Disability Discrimination Act (DDA) in December 1996, none of the employers contacted was aware of the Act or knew whether or not it applied to them (two of the three employers interviewed were subject to the Act):

> "Lack of awareness of the provisions of the law itself is not unexpected. The employment provisions of the Act were publicised at the time of introduction, but the overall impact of this major legislative change may have been diluted by the policy decision to gradually stage the introduction of the DDA's other provisions over the years ahead... little attention had been given to publicising and enforcing the quota requirements of the act which the DDA replaced, and it was not unexpected that employers knew nothing of those. (UK national report).

There is no specific provision for the enforcement of this legislation. Nor does the Act offer any financial incentives. The legislation remains untested at the time of this study. Unlike similar legislation around sex and race discrimination, there is no independent statutory body empowered to take investigative and, if necessary, legal action on behalf of people who believe that they have suffered discrimination on the basis of their disability. Cases brought by people on income levels such as those of economically inactive people with disabilities would seem unlikely without the intervention of a support organisation.

Attempts to introduce anti-discrimination legislation (covering both employment and access to services) in Ireland failed at the end of the study period in 1997 when, amongst other factors, key passages relating to workplace adaptations for people with disabilities were found to be unconstitutional as they infringed employers' property rights. Enforcement action was envisaged to be facilitated by an enlarged Employment Equality Agency. The two relevant Acts (Employment Equality Act and Equal Status Act) were approved by the Oireachtas (Parliament) but failed when referred to the Irish Supreme Court.

Employment Quotas

Under the Dutch law on work for disabled employees (WAGW), a non-compulsory quota of 5% of disabled employees was introduced. Normally, state the Dutch research team,

"little attention is paid to this quota in the business world, because there are no sanctions for companies who do not conform to it. This measure, which was introduced (but never ratified) around the time of the application procedure in case [Netherlands] 1, was seen as a positive step by this candidate. The introduction of the quota meant that disabled candidates from outside the company could be considered prior to the usual internal search for candidates... However, experience with this measure in the Netherlands in general indicates that it has no effect on the recruitment of employees with a disability." (Dutch national report).

In Spain, where two of the three cases were subject to the quota scheme, the system was sometimes similarly used to justify other motives:

"With regard to the legal obligation for 2% of the employees of companies with more than 50 employees to be people with a disability, employers are fully aware that this commitment is not worth the paper it is written on, since virtually no employer meets the standard and thus has no consequences, but they use it as an additional argument for strengthening their "model" policy of hiring some workers with disabilities (who in no case make up 2% of the staff)...In none of the three cases was there an official policy of promoting employment for people with disabilities, although in both case no. [Spain] 1 and case no. [Spain] 2, the enterprise did make an unwritten decision to hire people with disabilities until they reached the target of at least 2% of their staff." (Spanish national report)

In France and Germany, too, where one in three cases were in each country subject to the quota, this legislation was not thought likely, by national research teams, to have a great impact on recruitment practices. In France, despite the contributory role of the quota in case 2:

"For small enterprises, disability is not a burning issue. Either they are exempt from the employment obligation and do not hear anything about the matter or they are affected by it, in which case it is but one of the numerous constraints that complicate the management of their business, but seeking information on the subject will not constitute a priority." (French national report).

In Germany, where employers with less than 16 employees are not covered by the legislation, "'filling the quota' did not in itself constitute a reason for recruiting new disabled workers, and was only marginally relevant in combination with other factors." The national research team comment that discussion about the success of the quota revolves, in Germany, about the level of the penalty applied:

"Where employers in small firms have no other reasons for taking disabled workers on, they are not likely to change their staffing policy (or preconceptions) for the sake of saving DM 7200 per year (assuming a workforce of 50 and a compensatory levy of DM 200 x 3 people x 12 months.) For this reason the representatives of the self-help organisations have repeatedly called for a substantial increase in the compensatory levy. The current debate on subsidiary labour costs in Germany makes such an increase extremely unlikely, however." (German national report).

Registration

Mandatory employment protection and quota schemes appear to be commonly linked to registration schemes. Registration has been seen as unpopular in Britain, where the practice has now ceased, reflecting the negative personal and societal attitudes towards self-identification as having a disability and the absence of benefit deriving from registration. In France "the system for granting recognition as a disabled worker and the specialized training bodies came in for harsh criticism":

"Under the present French system for assisting disabled persons, this recognition opens the door to entitlements. Sometimes found to be a humiliating experience, the examination by COTOREP does not bring the disabled person any immediate benefits. Is it legitimate to preselect beneficiaries like this? The debate is still going on. Its advocates consider that it allows aid to be channelled towards those who really need it. Its adversaries maintain that it unnecessarily encumbers the process of allocating aid, an encumbrance for which a price has to be paid. It also marginalizes people who, despite having a rather inconspicuous disability, are really in need of assistance." (French national report).

Protection against Dismissal

Employees with disabilities in Germany enjoy a form of protection that is unique among the Member States studied. Under the Schwerbehindertengesetz (Severely Disabled Persons Act) employers are required to apply to the central welfare office for permission to dismiss an employee with a disability "once an indefinite employment relationship has lasted for longer than six months." Noting that the protection provides employees with job security, the German research team state that employers have different attitudes towards the measure depending on their previous experiences with it:

"Of the employers we interviewed those who had never been involved in such a procedure did not regard the protection as a problem. Those who had experience of protection procedures regarded it as a risk factor when deciding whether or not to employ a disabled worker. They perceived the extra interference in their management prerogatives by the central welfare office and the upheaval caused by the protection procedure as a problem, and it was even worse if it went to proceedings before an industrial tribunal." (German national report).

A significant part of this concern appeared to be due to the way in which they were informed about the measure before taking on an employee:

"Our survey showed that employers need to be given much clearer information on what the protection laws involve. The fact that they knew so little about the labour law situation was partly due to the fact that the officials responsible for placing disabled workers were deliberately vague on this point in the hope of "selling disabled workers as a low-risk undertaking". The reason given for this was that the target group had to compete not just with the able-bodied but also with the long-term and older unemployed." (German national report).

As a consequence, the advisory bodies "are often unaware of any problems until the application for dismissal is made." (German national report). Coupled with this, the low penalties for quota non-compliance and a harsher economic climate in Germany meant that protected jobs were being reserved for people who develop (or who might develop) a disability while they are employed by a company, rather than creating opportunities for the recruitment of people with disabilities.

"The quota and protection against dismissal therefore tend to help to secure existing jobs rather than to promote the integration of the disabled or to have a direct impact on the labour market." However: "Since concern about this special protection is rarely the only reason for not employing disabled workers, it seems likely that the job security benefits outweigh the deterrent effect on recruitment." (German national report).

The German research team concluded that the measure acts as a disincentive to the recruitment of people with disabilities but does ensure that there is an independent assessment before an employee with a disability is dismissed. Employers:

"are more likely to be prepared to employ them if they know about the dismissal procedure and what it involves beforehand... "Shielding" employers by not providing them with full information would seem to be less than helpful as a counselling strategy... It is more likely that greater numbers of disabled workers would be integrated on the primary labour market if better information and motivation were provided for employers." (German national report).

Health and Safety and Insurance Regulations

Fears around safety were a major motivating factor in three of the four Irish case studies and several of the UK cases. In Ireland, two manufacturing companies listed it as their chief concern:

- Enterprise 1 feared that lack of concentration while operating a power drill would endanger both the employee and other staff. This fear was realised in their opinion in the case of one employee who was let go, partly because he lacked the necessary concentration. However, the other employee was judged to be able to concentrate well and they no longer worry about safety in his case.

- Similarly, Enterprise 3 feared the potential dangers of the power saws on the factory floor. This problem was not overcome in the case of one employee who, having severe sensory disabilities, would have needed constant supervision to ensure that he did not wander into the path of such machinery. This was the main reason that the employee was not kept on. The company had no safety concerns for the other employee, who has schizophrenia and works in the office.

- While Enterprise 2 did not mention safety as a concern, they did admit that they would not consider employing someone with epilepsy unless they were in a team situation. They believed it important, for safety reasons, to have someone around to assist the person should they have a seizure.

Safety issues are considered as a top priority in the manufacturing companies mentioned, for all staff. Apart from their concern for the employees themselves, other staff members may feel at risk. There are also cost implications if more supervision is required." (Irish national report).

These statements bore out the experience of Irish support agencies who were frequently advised by companies that they were unwilling to employ people with a disability for safety reasons. Health and safety issues were also mentioned by some of the British employers.

Sickness and Health Legislation

Disability is often perceived to be associated with sickness and, therefore, absenteeism. This factor is present in all Member States but, when combined with lower awareness of financial incentives, appears to impact more heavily in countries without an implemented employment quota.

The Dutch national research team identified two subsidies available to employers to "set employers' minds at rest about the negative effects they (apparently) expect from employing a person with a disability, for example, higher sick leave costs." (Dutch national report). The team noted that awareness and take-up of such forms of support among SMEs studied was negligible, and made reference to ZARA, a quantitative study of around 3,300 employers on absenteeism, working conditions, reintegration and incapacity for work.

The results of the ZARA study were in complete harmony with the findings of the Dutch case studies: businesses made almost no use at all of the state measures provided to promote re-integration. "Virtually no company had a recruitment policy that focused on the employment of people with a partial capacity for work..." Where a company did have such people on the payroll, "they were people who were already employed by the company when they became incapacitated" (Dutch national report). Due to new legislation on absenteeism and incapacity for work – particularly 'Wulbz' measures which have extended the continuation of wage payments in case of sickness – small and medium sized enterprises take on few or no employees with a disability from outside the company. Although the contributory factors are different, this appears to be similar in impact to the German protection from dismissal measures.

In case study Netherlands 3, the employee complained that mediation support to find work commenced only at a very late stage. The research suggested that this was related to the right of an employee to be re-integrated back into the same company during the first year of sickness, or a result of a constant succession of regulatory and institutional changes over the past few years which had not given employment mediation agencies time to adjust their working practices:

> "A disabled employee is rarely seen as the best candidate because the employer is afraid that the candidate would be of limited usefulness and have an unpredictable or high rate of absenteeism. This attitude has been intensified by the privatisation of Sickness Insurance provisions and the planned privatisation and differentiation of social security premiums in the legislation on incapacity for work." (Dutch national report).

In Ireland, too, sickness was perceived to be a major risk factor in taking on a person with a disability:

> "Their fears range from practical issues of health and safety for the person and their co-workers, possible insurance problems and possible extra costs due to sick leave requirements..." (Irish national report).

In Britain, the study found that part time work suited both employee and employers, in part as a means of reducing risk:

> "Low-paid and undemanding work, for limited hours, may suit some disabled people's needs temporarily, because of financial pressures on the household or as a route into world of work. Disabled people in the

study tended to have low expectations and to be willing to work at a job below their capacity." (UK national report).

Employers in the particular labour market studied were thought to depend on a supply of workers willing to accept low wages and low hours. In addition, it was seen to be to some employers' advantage to keep hours below the threshold at which National Insurance (social welfare) contributions become payable, to reduce employment costs. When pay levels were below the contribution threshold, employees were likely to have no rights to holiday or sickness pay.

Summary of Barriers to Employment and Good Practice

Type of Action	Barriers to Employment	Good Practice
Financial incentives for employees	Transition into employment can result in financial disincentives rather than incentives in situations either when net income reduces or, if the transition is unsuccessful, when return to previous benefits is put in question	
Financial incentives for employers	Interview support measures appear misdirected unless accompanied by long term support measures; Premiums may have a negative effect on employee, employer and workplace relations, and lose sight of the key recruitment objective	Wages subsidies can act as clear compensation for any added supervision costs or reduced productivity; State insurance and related exemptions are favoured because they reduce implementation costs
Aids and Adaptations	Bureaucratic and inconsistent approaches between agencies can disadvantage the potential or existing employee	Approaches that view workplace aids and adaptations as necessary to ensure continued employment and business success can promote and maintain employment
Anti-Discrimination legislation	Lack of clear and supported mechanisms for enforcement; Applies only to firms over a certain size	Allows for reasonable adjustments to the workplace

Summary of Barriers to Employment and Good Practice *(continued)*

Type of Action	Barriers to Employment	Good Practice
Employment Quotas	Linked registration requirements can be seen as negative and humiliating; Apply to firms only over a certain size, limiting applicability to SMEs	Do not appear to be effective in themselves, but appear to be associated with higher awareness of accompanying financial incentive measures
Protection against Dismissal	Act as a disincentive to the recruitment of people with disabilities; Limited information is made available to employers regarding this measure by employment offices, who can be deliberately vague. Employers with experience of protection procedures regarded it is a significant risk	Ensure that there is an independent assessment before an employee with a disability is dismissed
Health and Safety legislation	Health and safety fears, and insurance costs are, unchecked, a major disincentive for employers	
Sickness and Health legislation	Disability is often perceived to be associated with sickness and absenteeism, and therefore higher staffing and insurance costs	

Employee Characteristics

Employee situations and experiences differed according to a range of personal characteristics, including:

* The nature and severity of the disability;
* Employees' age;
* Employees' gender;
* Educational attainment;
* Confidence and self-esteem;
* Employee integration and development.

The Nature and Severity of the Disability

Employer behaviour and employee experiences can be associated with the nature and severity of a disability.

The German research team found that people with mental illnesses were less likely to use specialist state mediating organisations, more likely to use general placement agencies and experienced most negative attitudes from employers:

> "Although the level of support needed by the mentally ill varies greatly according to the individual, employers still appear to regard this as the group involving the greatest "residual risk"." (German national report).

In Ireland:

> "Both NRB and Worklink reported that the label schizophrenia carries such stigma in Ireland that it is particularly hard to place someone with this illness in employment. The image created by the media of people with schizophrenia being violent is one which is widely held in Irish society. The crucial role played by the personal experience of employers is evidenced in this study by the fact that Enterprise [Ireland]3 had no worries about employing a person with this diagnosis, as he has personal prior experience of people with this illness." (Irish national report)

The French researchers noted simply that "behavioural disorders" along with significant and clearly obvious disabilities are "another high-profile disability that is not accepted" by employers (French national report).

On the other hand, people with learning disabilities were often perceived to exhibit qualities that compensated for their disability, as both British and German case studies demonstrated:

> "People with learning disabilities were looked upon favourably if such people were known to be reliable workers in routine tasks and in a stable, undemanding working environment. Indeed, people with learning difficulties could be considered more productive in tasks which non-disabled employees would find boring." (UK national report).

> "Although they may have a very limited understanding of the tasks that their job involves and how to perform them, as well as problems with social behaviour in some cases, these workers also have their strong points. Employers single out qualities such as willingness to work, reliability, punctuality and helpfulness." (German national report).

Few of the case studies involved people with severe disabilities. Where these occurred, employees generally fell into two categories:

• people with learning disabilities, in repetitive and unskilled, low paid work, often subsidised;

• wheelchair users and other people with mobility disabilities working in companies providing healthcare services, such as nursing or care homes, which have to be fully or largely accessible due to the nature of their client group. Other premises tended to be inaccessible to wheelchair users.

The Irish study found some indications that the experiences of employees with more severe disabilities were not as positive as those reported by the people with disabilities interviewed:

> • "Enterprise 3, for instance, employed a person with **multiple sensory disabilities and a learning disability,** but a combination of factors led to his not being retained - the factory floor was too dangerous an environment for a person with severe sensory disabilities, the tasks were too varied for him to learn and the staff taunted him.
>
> • Both manufacturing enterprises emphasised the need for employees to be fit and able for heavy physical work on the factory floor, by implication ruling out anyone with a severe **physical disability.**
>
> • Enterprise 3, speaking about **epilepsy,** pointed to the danger that a person with epilepsy might have a seizure while lifting a pillar: 'they could perhaps work in the stores'. Enterprise 2 would take on a person with epilepsy who was on medication, but only to work in a team setting. Enterprise 4 said that there would be no problem if the NTDI thought them suitable to the task, the person were on medication and not likely to have an incident on the floor which would expose them in front of staff." (Irish national report)

The French researcher considered the reluctance to employ people with severe disabilities to be a consequence of the employers' desire for a disability to not impact upon the running of the business:

> "It is ... quite unlikely that a job in a small enterprise would be given to anyone whose handicap is so severe that it would entail special arrangements in the workplace and that it would limit the person's ability to perform the whole range of duties in the job description... The

reluctance that is frequently expressed by heads of small enterprises to have anything to do with the employment of disabled persons is actually a desire to ensure that disabilities do not interfere with business operations. That undoubtedly explains their marked preference for disabilities that cannot be seen - and occasionally their astonishment when they encounter such disabilities - and on the other hand their refusal to recruit, and sometimes even to contemplate recruiting, people with severe and spectacularly obvious disabilities." (French national report).

Similarly, in Germany, it was felt that:

"The particularly severely disabled or those with multiple disabilities such as the elderly disabled, the physically and mentally disabled and the mentally ill have little chance of finding a job without special financial assistance." (German national report).

Employees' Age

The age range of employees in each of the national studies was relatively narrow, most between 22 to 38, with only three interviewees over this age.

The characteristics of older and younger employees also differed. Of the three sole older employees (described as 'middle aged', 'early 40s' and '50s') the first two cases had mental illnesses and the third epilepsy with a slight hearing loss.

The majority of younger cases had learning disabilities, with a few people reporting mobility, progressive disabilities or mental illness.

The concentration of younger people is probably a reflection of the average age of people who have recently received support from mediation agencies subsequent to the completion of formal education and/or diagnosis of the disability. These are people who have completed a number of years of training and are now ready to be placed in employment.

In some cases, this may also reflect the youth of public support measures. For example, in Ireland the Employment Support Scheme is a recent innovation. In Britain, too, many publicly funded measures seeking to promote the employment of people with disabilities are relatively new in scope and function. In both of these countries, 'special schooling' may, until relatively recently, have limited the ability and aspirations of many early-diagnosed people with disabilities to seek employment.

Given the absence in many national studies of identifiable employees with disabilities working in small and medium sized enterprises, there must be questions noted about the prospects of older people with disabilities finding work.

Employees' Gender

Each of the six national studies demonstrates the constraints imposed on people with disabilities in breaking away from traditional gender-based expectations of suitable work. Without exception:

- the women that took part in case studies undertook jobs in caring organisations, cleaning or catering, or undertook administrative work;

- the men that took part undertook manual unskilled or semi-skilled work or, if qualified (generally prior to diagnosis) undertook skilled professional work.

In Ireland, where all four enterprises were either manufacturing based or required heavy physical work, each had an overwhelmingly male workforce, with male to female ratios ranging from 2:1 to 6:1. Factory-floor applications by women would have been problematic for two of these enterprises, and a third firm had negative previous experience:

- the enterprise in case Ireland 1 stated that employing women could present difficulties for them in terms of the language used by the existing, male employees and the adequacy of their toilet facilities;

- in case study Ireland 3, also manufacturing, the enterprise felt that the work, being of a physical, semi-skilled nature, was traditionally more geared towards men and that the clerical or sales end might be more appropriate for women with disabilities;

- three women with disabilities arising from head injuries who were placed in the enterprise in case study Ireland 2, did not stay for more than a few months "because, according to the owner, it was tough work and they were married with children and under pressure to be at home." (Irish national report)

These results clearly suggest that disability creates a significant additional barrier to women seeking to enter non-traditional roles or professions.

Educational Attainment

Education is acknowledged to have a close relationship with both employment potential and earnings potential. Similarly, people with disabilities are known to have lower levels of educational attainment. The degree to which the age and educational attainment profile of people with disabilities differs between those using mediating organisations and those in employment generally is not known. It may be that qualified people with disabilities are less likely to utilise mediating organisations and are therefore under-represented in this study. However, given the general educational profile of people with disabilities and the relative absence of identifiable role models and alternative methods of sourcing cases to study, this would seem unlikely.

Significantly, the mediating organisations interviewed identified the low level of educational attainment of people with a disability as a major barrier to accessing employment. According to one Irish respondent:

> "the vast majority of people with a disability have gone through the special educational system, a system which does not usually follow a second level curriculum. Children with a physical disability may have missed school through hospitalisation and were commonly sent to special schools, regardless of ability. Third level education is not a choice without a second level qualification. Thus, training is the main option for people with a disability." (Irish national report).

People with a disability have only latterly been identified as having legitimate employment and work-related aspirations. The Irish National Rehabilitation Board stated that less than 10% of their clients would have completed second level education. The only person in the study with both a disability and a professional qualification was diagnosed as having his disability subsequent to attaining his degree and diploma. In a labour market that is increasingly demanding higher level qualifications, the absence of second level qualifications imposes an additional layer of disadvantage.

The French study stated that, while specialist training centres were not viewed positively, they had a clear and necessary role:

> "The specialised training centres (including the occupational retraining centres (CRPs)) are regularly criticised in France. Some regard them as obsolete, others as veritable ghettos, but they have not been replaced by any real opening up of the mainstream training centres. Nevertheless, their results are by no means negligible. The fact remains that many disabled persons do not possess the level of prior knowledge required for entry into mainstream certificate courses. The problem persists." (French national report).

Case study Netherlands 3 presents a case where an individual failed to complete a third level course due to the impact of his mental illness. His studies have subsequently been limited to short-term vocational training courses.

This low standard of educational attainment obviously further limits the range of opportunity open to people with disabilities, even in situations where supportive recruitment and employment practices are in place. The indirect result of this situation is that people with disabilities are competing for low wage, low skill jobs for which there is often little demand and high competition.

The British case material indicated that people with disabilities who are keen to work may be willing to take low-paid work below their capacity and adjust their hours of work to labour market requirements. However, an additional constraint in the British and Irish context lies in benefits systems which limit extra income from work or impose discontinuation risks. Where living with a disability imposes travel and other costs greater than the norm, low paid employment will not hold many attractions or benefits.

Confidence and Self-Esteem

The French researchers felt that managing a disability could provide a positive example of a person's ability:

> "The much-sought-after "extra" brought to the enterprise, apart from competence, may be the particularly high level of motivation demonstrated in the performance of their duties by disabled persons who have decided to take up employment. The difficulties they normally encounter before being recruited, in terms of either the effects of their disability or the long struggle to find a job, have often shaped their character in a way that makes them an example to other employees." (French national report).

In most case studies, however, having a disability was associated with low self-esteem and lack of confidence. In Ireland, only one of the six employees interviewed reported having looked for work on his own behalf, and this was the person with third level education and whose illness was only diagnosed in 1991:

> "Two of the employees said that they lacked the confidence to do so, were afraid they would be made a fool of, while four referred to the negative attitude of employers towards people with an illness... Several respondents commented on how difficult it is to 'keep applying for work' when you are so frequently refused an interview on the basis of

your disability. There is also the perception that, with unemployment so high among the general population, there is little hope for someone with a disability." (Irish national report)

In none of the Irish or British case studies did an enterprise reported having had an application from a person with a disability on their own behalf. In only one case (Germany 2) did an employee secure their job without the support of an intermediary.

In Britain, the research process highlighted the reluctance of employed people with disabilities to identify themselves in such a way: disability is not seen or accepted in any state as a positive form of self-identification. There was no response, for example, either to a local newspaper advertisement seeking to source case study material or to employer-distributed invitations to participate.

In the Netherlands, there were two cases where people with disabilities were sought for work. In each, the employers provided healthcare services which meant that they were familiar with the impact on work of their employees' disabilities.

Employee Integration and Development

In the Spanish case studies 1 and 2, there is a very clear link between the disability and the manner and extent to which the employees have been able to integrate. In case study Spain 2:

> "With regard to his relationship with colleagues, the initial communication problems have gradually been overcome and the worker with a disability can now address himself to any of his colleagues (with signs and mumbles), with no need for the mediation of the sponsor as happened initially. Nevertheless, as also occurred in case no. 1, there is a degree of *asymmetry* inasmuch as our employee has been marginalized/has marginalized himself from the usual channels of participation and management of his section in the enterprise (regular meetings at which everyone expresses a point of view about the enterprise's progress, makes proposals and so on). After attending a few of these meetings, his difficulty in following the content of debates led him to cease attending them" (Spanish national report).

This situation had two significant consequences, accentuating the employee's dependency on both the mediator and on decision-making processes regarding which he was unable to contribute. Effective guidance and support by their manager and/or colleagues is required to improve performance and integrate into a company. A hearing and speech impairment combined with a low level of educational attainment to reduce the employee's flexibility and adaptability to new work:

> "...the section head who acts as "sponsor" or guardian for the person concerned stresses the specific limitations that a hearing/speech impairment imposes, inasmuch as it makes *communication* more difficult, thereby reducing the *flexibility* to do new work or introduce changes to customary procedures. This consideration does not imply a negative assessment of the worker, but recognition of some specific limitations in relation to the ideal model of a competitive worker. However, in addition, we have in this case [Spain 2] the limitation of the *low level of education* (another common characteristic of people with disabilities in Spain), which cannot be attributed directly to the disability, but which reinforces and aggravates the problem of communication (great difficulty in written language and using the computer terminals that the enterprise has introduced into all sections)." (Spanish case study).

Poor integration can also be attributed to a lack of confidence or self-esteem. Irish case study 3 demonstrates the importance of self-esteem and confidence in developing work relationships and promoting career progression:

> "Enterprise 3 was disappointed that the employee has not integrated more as this would increase his chance of being kept on. And this was linked by the manager to the employee's reluctance to widen his skills base. People at his level are expected to diversify and to nurture promotional prospects." (Irish national report).

In the Spanish case, as with the Irish example, the extent to which an employee has effectively integrated only comes at the expiration of any financial assistance, or in times of economic downturn:

> "Once the financial assistance paid for employing a disabled worker expires, the job is covered by a further period of grace, since [in Spain] if the employment relationship with the disabled worker is terminated within a year of the expiry date the assistance must be reimbursed. Only after this period does it become clear whether integration has really been successful. Regardless of whether the employment relationships have continued, most of the nineteen employers interviewed said that they would take on disabled workers in the future." (Spanish national report).

Summary of Barriers to Employment and Good Practice

Characteristic	Barriers to Employment	Good Practice
The nature and severity of the disability	People with severe disabilities are particularly disadvantaged, as are people with mental illnesses	People with learning disabilities are sometimes regarded as more suitable to undertake some tasks, such as those involving a high degree of repetition
Employees' age	Few examples of older people with disabilities in employment, suggests that age may constitute a barrier	
Employees' gender	There is a clear indication that disability creates a significant additional barrier to women seeking to enter non-traditional roles or professions	
Educational attainment	Strong association between disability and low levels of educational attainment and therefore employment and earnings potential	
Confidence and self-esteem	Lack of self-esteem and confidence is common to people with disabilities, with consequences in seeking employment	
Employee integration and development	Lack of self-esteem and confidence has consequences in maintaining employment	

Employer and Workplace-Related Characteristics

Employer and workplace-related characteristics having an influence on the employment of people with disabilities are:

* Workplace organisation and decision making;

* Recruitment practices;

* Attitudes towards disability, including perceptions of risk and social awareness;

- Enterprise trade sector

- Employment terms and conditions;

- Employee representation;

- Workspace accessibility.

Workplace Organisation and Decision Making

Work Organisation

National teams differed marginally in their analysis of the impact of company size on the propensity of an enterprise to recruit people with disabilities. In the Irish study:

> "There are no figures available, but the feeling of those working in placement agencies is that, apart from large companies with stated Equal Opportunities policies, the smaller company is much more likely to employ someone with a disability.... One agency thought that smaller companies who do not offer many commitments to their staff regarding sick leave and other benefits can be more willing to take a chance with an employee as they have less to risk." (Irish national report).

The British research team found that: "Much more relevant than size is flexibility in the organisation of labour." (UK national report). Both of the situations described in the Irish and British examples arise from the same characteristic of small and medium sized enterprises. Rather than broad labour market flexibility (although this might well be seen as advantageous by many small and medium sized enterprises), this characteristic revolves around the manner in which work is organised in small enterprises, with a greater need for work flexibility, independent, self-directed working and multiskilling.

> "Complete independence in the workplace, including the ability to move unaided to and from amenities such as the toilets and canteen, is often ... advanced as a condition sine qua non.

> "Similarly, while employees in a large company are so interchangeable as to have given birth to the well-worn cliché that nobody is irreplaceable, the situation is very different in a small business. Every employee has a part to play which is indispensable to the proper functioning of the whole operation." (French national report).

Such flexibility is likely to be more commonly demanded in small and medium sized enterprises than in larger organisations with greater job specialisation (and organised labour). While many legal requirements in most Member States are not applicable to smaller enterprises, perhaps reducing some (overall, perhaps not proportional) compliance or implementation costs, the same range of tasks and functions need to be carried out in every business, regardless of size. In SMEs, these are carried out by fewer people. The fewer the number of people in an enterprise, the greater will be the number and range of production and administration tasks they are each likely to have to undertake.

An employee with a disability might need adjustments to working hours, rest periods, work tempo and content. The British researchers note that:

> "adapting the way the work is organised depends on the co-operation of other staff, whose social or financial rewards may be adversely affected by changes to working arrangements. An important decision-making factor in recruitment was how the applicant 'fitted in', both with the requirements of the job and with co-workers. Changing the job to meet the requirements of the applicant may require 'disability awareness' on the part of employees as well as the employer. Even if the other employees were willing to work around the needs of a disabled employee, in small firms such adaptations could threaten the viability of the enterprise, if overall productivity were reduced." (UK national report).

For many small businesses, the ability to alter work processes or methods may be limited and it may not be possible to design a full time job that takes full account of the impact of a disability.

The textile factory in case UK 2 operated a finely tuned co-operative system, which could be reorganised only with great difficulty and at some cost, limiting opportunities to create positions to suit people with a disability. At the other end of the scale, the nursing home in case UK 3 required staff with a broader range of skills. Working hours were more flexible, and individuals could be found positions to suit their circumstances.

> "One of the legitimate concerns that employers have is the special support that certain disabilities require at work, which may mean that previously established work processes need to be redesigned." (German national report)

> "...stress levels were conspicuously high in the three small enterprises where we conducted our survey. There are two reasons for this: on the one hand, their survival will not be assured in the highly competitive

world in which they operate (it is always possible that someone, from one day to the next, will set up a business and take away some of their custom) unless a brisk working rhythm and constant readiness to respond to the unexpected are maintained; on the other hand, since each new employee represents a significant quantum leap for them, they tend to be understaffed, which means that each employee is burdened with a heavier workload more frequently and perhaps for longer periods than in larger enterprises." (French national report).

The manager of the enterprise in case study Ireland 2 felt that employees with a learning disability are often unable to take the initiative, to notice for themselves what needs doing. Consequently, greater supervision was needed, with extra cost implications. In case Ireland 1, the manager stated that higher levels of skills are now required in the business. The implied concern was that people with a disability might not have such skills.

The level of supervision or coaching required is entirely dependent upon the nature of the disability that an employee experiences, but might in many situations be sufficiently intensive that the time and cost of such needs should be carefully considered in staff planning.

Decision Making

In addition to the need for multi-skilled and customer-oriented staff, a small or medium sized enterprise will be managed very differently to larger businesses. Hierarchies will tend to be flat (necessitated, if for no other reason, by the number of employees) and management styles more informal and face-to-face.

For example, for small companies, the decision to employ someone can usually be done quickly and by one person. The manager of a small company is personally motivated to employ someone and can do so without reference to others. In the Dutch specialised cleaning services case (Netherlands 2), the applicant with a disability was able to impress her enthusiasm and strong motivation upon the owner such that he commented:

> "In our estimation, it would have been far more difficult for the disabled people described here to secure a job through a normal selection procedure in competition with other candidates. In many cases their disability will put them at a disadvantage." (Dutch national report).

In Britain, France, Ireland and the Netherlands, informal recruitment processes benefited applications from people with disabilities and their promoters. Significantly, the participation of senior management staff in all stages of the recruitment process offered distinct advantages in recruitment terms. People with a disability (and their promoters) can gain fast and direct access to decision makers:

"When placement agents contact a small business, they deal with the head of the business. He is the one who will take the decision, and he is able to assess the feasibility of the project himself, whereas in the case of large enterprises a disagreement between the personnel manager and the managing director, or between the latter and his board, can derail the whole operation. In addition, although it never happens in large companies, the owner of a small business will be in direct touch with the disabled person he decides to employ and will work with that person. He is better placed to assess the newcomer's chances of integration into the existing team, but by the same token he will also be held personally responsible for failure if integration does not take place or if the disabled person does not accept the duties assigned to him." (French national report).

The same decision-making factors also improve the chances of successful responses to approaches by mediating organisations:

"It is also possible for placement agencies to build up a relationship with smaller companies – most of the enterprises which we interviewed had taken on more than the one person with a disability from the agency they dealt with. This flexibility is not seen in larger companies it seems, unless they developed a specific policy regarding disability equality." (Irish national report).

Recruitment Practices

The Application Process

Small and medium sized enterprises tend, in each Member State, to have informal and ad hoc recruitment processes. Unsurprisingly, the smaller the company, the less structured the process. Formal procedures are more suited to larger enterprises, with greater and more frequent need for recruitment and greater job specialisation.

"Small independent firms tend not to look for workers until they are totally overloaded and can no longer do the work themselves, and then they will certainly not think of taking on a disabled worker. They are not recruiting to meet some sort of staffing programme, but because they cannot do the work." (German national report).

The impact of this informality and lack of structure on applicants with disabilities is mixed. Where enterprises have no formal recruitment policy or practices, they are unlikely to formulate procedures promoting equality of opportunity for people with disabilities or, indeed, any other group. The British research team noted that "Small businesses in a competitive market have few links with other enterprises where they might discover 'good employment practices'." Nor, the British team state,

> "is there necessarily any incentive to be seen as 'positive about disabled people'. When filling job vacancies the employers did not actively try to attract applications from disabled people or guarantee interviews to all disabled applicants who met the minimum criteria... It is not apparent why they should wish to do so, with no obvious business advantage attached, although disabled staff could portray a positive image of a caring enterprise, particularly appropriate where the commodity was care." (UK national report).

The most common recruitment methods used by small and medium sized enterprises included: personal recommendations, family and friendship connections with existing or previous employees, speculative enquiries and only then the use of state recruitment agencies. Most vacancies are filled without advertising and, where this approach is adopted, it is often informal, such as through notices in small local shops. Where a job is advertised, and particularly if it needs to be filled quickly or the field is limited, it is often given to the first good applicant who meets the criteria for the vacancy.

In every case, employers balanced the perceived disadvantages attached to employing people with a disability against the perceived advantages their skills and experience would bring.

> "In small enterprises, indeed, disability is obscured - not really concealed, but overlooked. It is not one of the factors taken into account by the enterprise, not even in the context of personnel management. That does not mean that the employer refuses to consider it but rather that he trivializes it and that he would not generally wish it to interfere with his company's operations" and "When employers are asked for the reasons that led them to employ disabled persons, they always emphasize first and foremost the abilities of these candidates and the fact that they needed someone with the candidate's qualifications, irrespective of the disability." (French national report).

"Many employers point out that every worker needs to "pull his own weight", particularly in small firms, and they stress that certain cases require 100% financial assistance or else payment of a permanent underperformance allowance." (German national report).

When recruiting, it is rare for any employer to decide to give preference to an applicant because they have a disability. Such cases, examples of which there are in Ireland (Ireland 2), the Netherlands (Netherlands 1 and 3) and Spain (Spain 3), appear to be motivated by a range of factors, including a philanthropic motive, but also the existence of possible subsidies (Ireland and Spain), direct or indirect personal contact, new quota legislation (Netherlands) and a desire to promote a positive and caring image. Some employers and researchers expressed concerns that work demands could adversely affect the well-being of a potential employee:

"In the situations we have analysed, we cannot really gauge the extent to which the disabled employees will be able to withstand the pressure... For some disabled employees, the stress and the pace of work seem to be a source of fatigue. It may be thought that if a person's disability makes that person more vulnerable physically, which our past surveys suggest is not an unusual phenomenon, this type of climate would be rather more likely to aggravate the disability and weaken the will to work than to encourage permanent employment." (French national report).

Application Forms

The use of application forms, which frequently ask about the health or disability status of the applicant when they are legally able, is less prevalent in the small and medium sized enterprise sector. The absence of such questions was considered by national researchers in Ireland to "make it easier for persons with a disability to secure an interview without reference to their disability."

In a similar vein, noting the use of medical or disability-related information to filter applicants, also in Ireland: "One employee reported that going through a recruitment agency, the norm in his field, meant that he did not have to fill out any forms before getting to interview, a distinct advantage for him." (Irish national report).

Application forms, if used, may ask about the health or disability status of the applicant in Ireland and Britain. In the Irish case study experience, this can diminish the possibility of getting to interview. One expert validating the case study material reported that, of 85 recent applications made, only one had resulted in an interview.

In Ireland, half of the four enterprises studied used formal application forms which asked about health or disability of applicant as this affected the insurances required by the company to trade legally. Applicants to the other two Irish companies gave their personal details over the telephone, on the basis of which they were called to interview, a procedure which may make it easier for some people with disabilities to secure an interview without making reference to their disability:

> "However, the reality is that none of the employers reported ever having received an application from a person with a disability through conventional recruitment channels. " (Irish national report).

For employees with cyclical or periodic disabilities, such as some forms of mental illness or Multiple Sclerosis, or those requiring hospitalisation, gaps in their work patterns can arise which become apparent in their curriculum vitaes. In case study Ireland 3, this was a major concern in interviews for the person with schizophrenia, and meant that questions about his disability could not be avoided. In his case, the norm in the employee's field was to secure employment through a recruitment agency, meaning that he did not have to complete any forms before getting to interview, a distinct advantage. The job he secured, however, did not arise in this manner, casting doubt on the success of such an approach. One such agency advised one of the Irish employees that "companies do not like people who have been sick" (Irish national report).

Making a Disability Visible

The Dutch research team noted that:

> "employers consider it to be important that candidates place more emphasis on what they can do than on what their physical or mental disability prevents them from doing. At the same time, making no mention at all of an (invisible) disability during the selection process or medical assessment can lead to considerable problems with work relations later, and may even be a reason for immediate dismissal." (Dutch national report).

Similarly, in the British case studies:

> "Employers did not expect to raise the matter of health status or disability. Of foremost importance to the employer were the applicant's skills and ability to do the job, when vacancies were hard to fill. Applicants were made fully aware of the physical demands and stresses of the work and were thus expected to rule themselves out if the job was

beyond them. Consequently, adjustments which might help someone to do the job on equal terms were not discussed. Moreover, as mental illness and the general effects of ageing were not automatically recognised as disabilities, the effects of hidden or unacknowledged disability were not considered." (UK national report).

Some Irish employees had the perception that, if prospective employers knew of their disability, they would not be taken on. An Irish employee with a learning disability stated that an interview would be going well until the employer saw the name of a specialist organisation supporting people with learning disabilities in his curriculum vitae. At this point, the employer lost interest. The Irish National Rehabilitation Board state that "personnel officers are not trained to raise the issue of disability in a positive way: they either ignore it or deal with it in a negative way." (Irish national report).

The existence of a medical test could be seen as another barrier to accessing employment. Medical testing may, for example, uncover information that is not relevant to a job but which may have a consequence on an employee's perceived suitability. While most case studies gave little evidence of this as either a barrier or example of good practice, this is not surprising as most employers were aware that they were employing someone with a disability and the recruitment exercises had been successful. Nevertheless, while none of the four Irish enterprises required medical tests, both of the two manufacturing enterprises were about to introduce testing in order to establish baseline records regarding their health, and particularly focused on hearing. This was undertaken not to exclude people with hearing problems, but in order to prevent litigation by employees on the grounds that their workplace had caused such problems: "One enterprise stated that they are saving £20,000 per annum in insurance costs by introducing such tests." (Irish national report).

Attitudes towards Disability

Perceptions of Risk

"There are far more similarities than differences in the experience of people with disabilities seeking employment. The common barrier to employment which all people with disabilities have to overcome is the negative attitude of prospective employers to disability." (Irish national report).

All mediating organisations – and other bodies interviewed in Ireland – reported negative attitudes of employers as the most significant barrier to employment. This was described by the state National Rehabilitation Board as "a lack of knowledge and information regarding disability which caused employers to make decisions based on myths and false perceptions".

> "The Production Manager in one company said that another person with responsibility for hiring people might take the view that a person with a disability is an extra liability to be avoided. Many of these fears, apart from showing a negative image of people with disabilities, seem to have to do with the fear of the unknown." (Irish national report).

In the case of schizophrenia, there is an additional "prejudice arising from the negative portrayals in the media of people with this illness" (Irish national report). This particular focus on mental health was noted also by the Dutch research team: "Companies are slightly more wary of people with mental illnesses than of those with physical disabilities; they see the former as less predictable", however:

> "The smaller enterprises generally indicated that they did not wish to run any risk at all, mainly for organisational reasons. It is clear that employers are strongly influenced by a negative view of disabled employees in this respect, since a work disability need not go hand in hand with higher absenteeism or lower productivity. The three cases described give examples of employers who focus more on a disabled person's capabilities than on his or her limitations." (Dutch national report).

> "Highly dependent on the availability of their workforce to respond to the constantly changing work patterns of their enterprises, the interviewed employers generally expressed the need for regularity. Unforeseen absenteeism is their greatest fear. That is why they will refuse outright to employ people whose disability could create a climate of uncertainty or result in unforeseeable absences." (French national report).

Prospective employers fear that the person with a disability will be a liability, an extra problem to the company. Their fears range from practical issues of health and safety for the person and their co-workers, possible insurance problems and possible extra costs due to sick leave requirements, to perceptions of the person with a disability as unable to integrate with co-workers, to take the initiative, to deal with pressure and to progress within the company. These perceptions are based on a lack of knowledge about disability, exacerbated by the general lack of integration into mainstream society.

The level of risk perceived in taking on a person with a disability clearly affects the outcome of the recruitment process. Weighing up the costs and benefits is a process that is not necessarily conducted with clear and objective criteria: it will incorporate subjective perceptions of ability and disability.

On the cost side, an employer will take into account the monetary cost of physical and work process adaptations: a person with a disability is more readily taken on if any adaptations required to the workplace and work processes are simple, easily identifiable and low in cost.

General concerns about the profitability of the business are of equal importance. Particularly where a business is small, new or active in a volatile market, employing a person with a disability would represent an additional risk in an already precarious financial situation. Where the business – or its market – is in a period of growth and is reasonably profitable, the management may feel more inclined to take risks:

> "In the case of the current employee, issues are recognised around integration into the workforce. The manager in this case felt that the employee might suffer through isolation or redundancy if he found it difficult to diversify in his work and develop his capabilities: where a person is not able to progress and diversify, a question will be raised in the longer term as to the profitability of retaining them, particularly if salaries increase annually. In this company, while it is performing well, staff positions are secure, but the industry is volatile and only three years ago significant cutbacks were made. Training and support measures should therefore take account of this need to develop." (Irish national report: case study 3).

Nevertheless, as reported by the British and German research teams, supporting existing long-term employees who become ill or disabled may take priority over taking on new staff with a disability.

Despite these fears, no case study employees reported discrimination by their employers. Quite the reverse was the case - many reported a high level of support from their employer. This is not surprising as the employers studied have been motivated to successfully employ a person with disability. This finding is contrary to the expectations of support agencies for people with a disability who, in Ireland for example, report employers' negative attitudes as the chief barrier to employment for people with a disability, based on a lack of knowledge about disability. That the attitude of employers is a major factor regarding the employment of people with disabilities is borne out in case studies in each Member State.

Personal Experience of Disability

In a significant number of cases, the person with responsibility for employing people with disabilities had a personal experience of someone with a disability. Of 19 employers, 8 (42%) had some personal experience of people with disabilities outside their current employment (a further 7 (37%) stated some motive based on social awareness or social obligation). This personal experience was frequently stated as the primary motivation for employing such a person: they had no misconceptions about disability because of their experience and they also wished to "give a person a chance":

> "Unless you have personal contact with a person with a disability you will not understand what is involved." (Production Manager, case study Ireland 3).

Overall, the breakdown of stated reasons related to previous experience is as follows:

Basis of Employers' Attitudes to Disability

Attitude Type	France	Germany	Ireland	NL	Spain	UK*	%	Total
Personal Experience	2	1	3	1		1	42%	8
Family background		1	2					3
Previous employment	2		1			1		4
Personal knowledge of applicant				1				1
Social awareness		1	1	2	2	1	37%	7
Other	1	1			1	1	21%	4
Total	3	3	4	3	3	3	100%	19

* UK employer interviews only: case study material without employer interviews is excluded.

In all three cases in the Netherlands there was a director who was concerned about the situation of the person with a disability in question and wanted to give them an opportunity.

> "Coaching and support on the job was important in all cases. The employee in case 1 was "shown the ropes" by a friend outside working

hours. In cases 2 and 3 the employees were coached by their director to help them learn the work, which was new to them. In case 3 this took place once a week, and in addition the employee could rely on extra work support from the project's advisory committee... The medical and paramedical support (ergotherapist, rehabilitation specialist) on hand in the workplace in case 1 made a valuable contribution to the provision of a suitable working environment and the correct equipment." (Dutch national report)

In case Netherlands 3, it was significant that both of the employee's post-diagnosis employers were institutions within or linked to mental healthcare. Similarly, in Germany:

"Employers consider employing disabled workers if they already have an affinity with the disabled, for instance if they themselves, members of their families or their friends are disabled or have disabled children, or if they already have disabled workers in the firm. Otherwise the firm must be introduced to the idea." (German national report).

These characteristics show the concrete value of knowledge of disability in overcoming discrimination arising from negative attitudes towards disability.

Social Awareness

With the possible exception of the French study, national studies consistently identified the issues of enterprises' social awareness or concern about projecting a social image. These concerns were typically associated with business location or trade sector. In the British cases, all urban:

"Selection was not influenced by charitable motives, by a desire to support disabled people's rights to employment or by a wish to project a positive image... Nor is there necessarily any incentive to be seen as 'positive about disabled people'... It is not apparent why they should wish to do so, with no obvious business advantage attached, although disabled staff could portray a positive image of a caring enterprise, particularly appropriate where the commodity was care." (UK national report).

The possibilities of a caring approach were documented in cases in both the Netherlands and Ireland. The first Dutch case study involved a healthcare institution in a small village community. Not only did readily accessible premises and a familiarity with health and disability issues affect the recruitment decision:

"This location entails a greater degree of social involvement than would be the case in an urban area. The director of the institution had heard about the applicant's past accident and was prepared to do something for her as a fellow-villager. Apart from this social concern, the effect on the institution's image among the local inhabitants will also have played a part in his decision to employ a disabled person." (Dutch national report).

The Irish research team also noted that social image aspect is more often a significant factor in recruitment policy in a rural or village environment than in an urban environment. While the electrical switch manufacturer in case study Ireland 1 "does not need to engage in a proactive programme of recruitment: 'Applications pour in from the local town'...", employing people with a disability:

"increases public faith in the company. The enterprise is located in a small community and 85% of employees are local. Both interviewees considered it to be an advantage to the company locally if it is 'seen to be looking after disabled people'." (Irish national report).

Amongst the stakeholders involved in case Spain 2:

"special mention should be made of the *leading role played by the enterprise* which, at a given moment, adopted a specific policy of hiring some people with disabilities, with a view to reaching at least the 2% target set by the law. This decision was prompted by the manager of the shopping centre, not by the company at multinational level, and the reason put forward by the interviewee (the manager's assistant) was that the manager had "special awareness" in this area. Consequently, as there were no job applicants with handicaps, the enterprise sought out organizations who could provide them ... Three people obtained jobs ... and two are about to obtain them ... Apart from the possible "personal" motives of the manager, which we do not know (perhaps he has somebody in the family with a disability), one of the theories we find most plausible is an *attempt to gain legitimization and a good social image* on the part of an enterprise whose profitability is primarily based on employing, for the most part, a casual, low-paid workforce (young students who receive an amount close to the minimum wage)." (Spanish national report).

The distinction between the more altruistic and the more image conscious concerns is heavily blurred and, ultimately unnecessary: most businesses would recognise themselves to be at some point between these two polar opposites.

Instances of empathy do, however, take place in both recruitment and job retention throughout the case studies:

> "Sympathetic employers or supervisors, who were sensitive to problems encountered and were willing to make suitable adjustments, prevented unnecessary job loss. For example, a supervisor had arranged for disabled workers to be moved to positions better suited to their disabilities. In another case, following confusion over the rules applying to ATW [financial support for workplace adaptations], the employer had himself paid for adaptations to the premises essential to maintain the individual's employment." (UK national report).

Particularly in the Spanish studies, terms such as "social responsibility" were mentioned, with a quite different emphasis to the more commonly stated term, "social awareness":

> "When they are pressed to indicate what other criteria should be put forward, the response is very general: having *"social awareness"*. This expression, which was used by both the manager and the guardian, reveals an attitude of pity or support for people suffering social disadvantage, rather than an acknowledgement of the *right of all citizens to work*, irrespective of their degree of efficiency" (Spanish national report).

This approach, whether philanthropic or opportunistic may have limitations. It is not clear from the case studies whether or not such attitudes can limit the type and nature of employment opportunities offered to people with disabilities. On the one hand, educational attainment levels tend to be low, but on the other hand, this factor is associated with the nature of a disability and its impact upon schooling opportunities. There is only a single example in the study of an employee with a disability who has a professional qualification.

Whether arising out of charitable or compassionate behaviour, it is likely that people perceived to be deserving of charity and a 'good cause' are less likely to be perceived to be able to do a job effectively. The consequence of charitable - and medical models of disability - is that people are separated out from mainstream society into special institutions and facilities. With this lack of integration, people with disabilities are made invisible, marginalised and not normal.

Staff Attitudes

Discrimination by employees appears to take two forms: direct discrimination on the basis of the person's characteristics, and indirect discrimination based upon necessary changes to workplace practices. The possibility of difficulties arising from staff relations in the workplace was a determining factor for some enterprises in the recruitment process.

While several employees reported being discriminated against by their fellow employees, in some cases this was clearly not related to the person's disability. Indeed, it was not always clear whether co-workers were aware of a person's disability.

In case study Ireland 3, staff members who knew of an employee's schizophrenia had feared that he might become violent. The company's Production Manager was able to allay their fears and there have been no significant staff relations problems for the employee, who remains unaware that his work colleagues know of his disability.

In Ireland, two case study employees reported difficulty with taunts by co-workers, in one case directly related to his disability: an employee in case study Ireland 3 was subjected to whispering and sniggering because of his poor speech. The manager of the enterprise felt that such behaviour could lead to staff disharmony and staff relations problems. It was sometimes thought difficult to determine whether the behaviour was motivated by prejudice or was part and parcel of normal working relationships and banter between workers. (Irish national report). In some previous employment cases, these were not resolved and the employment terminated.

In one instance in case study Ireland 4, an employee initially felt unable to deal with the taunting or 'slagging' that formed part of the usual working relationships between staff in the enterprise. In this case, although he reciprocated with others, he was sensitive to being targeted himself. With the support of his supervisor and a job coach from a mediating organisation he learned to cope with it.

Case studies also demonstrated other types of behaviour which, while not necessarily discriminatory, could be regarded as limiting. In the Spanish cases:

> "With regard to work colleagues, case no. 3 is the only one in the assistant category, which places him below and at the service of the other workers. They adopt a **"paternal" attitude towards him which is a result both of the age difference and his disabled status,** together with some specific problems in performing the work which are attributable to difficulty in remembering things, but which are probably related to his low level of intelligence and understanding of the

instructions he receives. Nevertheless, these are minor problems which do not substantially affect the performance of the tasks he has to carry out." (Spanish national report).

Adaptations to the organisation of work are also significant. The working hours were adjusted in two of the three Dutch cases (Netherlands 1 and 2). In case Netherlands 1 this was required due to the employee's stamina, but also because of the extra time it took the employee to use her toilet facilities and to get to and from work. This had consequences for her colleagues doing the same work, which led to difficult working relations in the beginning due to opposition from work colleagues. In this example:

"the working hours of all the telephonists had to be changed specially to accommodate their disabled colleague. After the director had spoken to all concerned, and once they had got to know their new colleague better, the problems disappeared. Later, according to the disabled employee, she even enjoyed excellent support from her colleagues." (Dutch national report).

As is the case with employers, some degree of personal experience or understanding of disability by employees is an important element in promoting successful integration. In case study Spain 1, work colleagues expressed more informed views than the employer:

"For the enterprise's personnel department, the prerequisite for hiring people with a disability is that they *should have a normal level of work efficiency* (in other words, like that of other people who have no disability) in relation to the job they are going to do. In our case, the manager thinks that the worker with Down's Syndrome performs as well as other potential candidates in the ancillary job he holds... On this point, the guardian and, according to her, his immediate work colleagues *do not share this opinion, but believe that such workers do have some specific limitations in comparison with most people without this form of disability, making them, overall, less efficient at work.* In particular, they are more easily distracted and require quite continuous and sympathetic (paternal) assistance or support from all their colleagues and, above all, from one of them explicitly entrusted with the task (in our case, the guardian). As far as colleagues are concerned, such support should not be an obstacle to hiring such people, because they understand that work performance should not be the only criterion taken into account in access to employment." (Spanish national report)

Customers' Attitudes

Instances where customers might discriminate were outlined only in the British and French studies. In the British study, two such circumstances were identified:

- "upset to other members of staff, or to customers, through inappropriate social behaviour

- "customer dissatisfaction if the employee could not meet the demands of the job" (UK national report).

In the French study, the manager of case France 2 believed that visible disabilities would be hard for the clients of medical clinic to handle. While not specifically mentioned in other case studies, fears of these reactions by customers are likely to have a significant bearing upon the attitude of employers to applicants during the recruitment process.

Enterprise Trade Sector

Not only is there is a prevalence of employees sourced through mediating organisations in the case studies, there is also a high percentage of businesses in the sample (almost 30%) providing caring services. Four of the six national studies included such cases and in two of these studies, they constituted two thirds of the cases examined. In addition, almost 50% of enterprises studied were manufacturing.

Case Study Enterprises by Trade Sector

Member State	Caring Services	Other Services	Total Services	Manu-facturing	Construction/ Engineering	Total
France	2		2	1		3
Germany	1		1	1	1	3
Ireland		1	1	3		4
Netherlands	2	1	3			3
Spain		1	1	2		3
UK	1	1	2	3	1	6
Total	6	4	10	10	2	22

While there is much scope for statistical error in such small samples, the prevalence of these types of enterprise across the study does seem to be significant.

The number of manufacturing enterprises may be primarily a factor unique to this sample and of only marginal significance: other factors such as business location and the severity of the employees' disabilities come into play. However, the repetitive nature of available factory-floor tasks may also be relevant. 50% (5) of the people with learning disabilities studied work for manufacturing businesses (a further 3 work in caring services and 2 in other services).

The prevalence of caring service enterprises appears to be linked to three factors: a familiarity with issues around health and disability; the greater likelihood of accessible premises; and the desire to demonstrate social awareness, as in the following Spanish example:

> "On the part of the enterprise hiring the worker, the main explicit motivation is its position as a charity: it not only acknowledges the legal obligation to fill the 2% quota, but feels it should give an example of "awareness" to other companies." (Spanish national report).

Employment Terms and Conditions

In situations where an applicant is being seriously considered for a vacancy, means of reducing the perceived risk attached to a disability through the use of non-permanent contracts can prove useful (although a return to state benefits might be affected in some countries if an ability to work is proven):

> "In [Dutch] cases 1 and 3, the disabled candidates were initially employed on a contract with a limited duration. Although the employers interviewed did not mention this argument, this entailed a lower risk for the employer: if the employee proved to be unsatisfactory or off sick too often, the contract could be terminated." (Dutch national report).

In Britain, income support measures for people with a disability mean that only part-time work, with restricted legal rights, may be feasible if they, or their partner, receive out-of-work social security benefits. However, at least temporarily, this can suit some job seekers.

A contrast, or even conflict, in expectations can arise in two areas: between the employer and the employee and between the employer and a mediating organisation. In case study Spain 2, only part time, low wage work was available for a person with a hearing disability, due in part to his educational attainment and ability. The motivation and aspirations of the employee were governed by other factors:

"The working environment in the new enterprise is satisfactory, but the income is very low for an adult wishing to settle down professionally (Ptas 40,000 net per month, 20 hours' work per week). In this context, the worker is at a decisive stage in his life, seeking to ensure settled employment in order to get married and set up his own home, independent of his parents. This means that he approaches his work with a great feeling of responsibility and a wish to do it properly and to the satisfaction of those in charge. For this reason, he is always prepared to work overtime, even on Sundays, and to co-operate in whatever is asked of him." (Spanish national report).

The German research team noted that:

"There are frequent disputes between employment offices and employers at the start of the employment relationship about the wages that the disabled worker is to be paid. Employers tend to look forward to the period following expiry of the financial assistance and steer clear of "inflated" wages. The welfare offices are currently assessing individual applications for underperformance allowances more critically than before and sometimes not granting them in full, on account of the rising number of applications and the restrictions on resources." (German national report).

Employee Representation

There were few indications in any Member State that trade unions or works councils played an active role on the issue of disability at SME company level.

"...small firms tend not to have disabled workers' representatives, works councils or employers' representatives, or if they do, they tend not to have the same institutional power as in larger firms. Communication and small, flexible support networks of "helpers" are more important here for both employers and disabled workers" (German national report).

Workspace Accessibility

Readily accessible premises play an important part in promoting access to employment for people with disabilities. In no country are there obligations for adaptations of old buildings to include reasonable improvements to accessibility as a matter of course.

Nursing homes and medical clinics in France, the Netherlands and the UK therefore provided opportunities for the employment of people with mobility disabilities. While, in the Dutch studies, the directors of the three enterprises studied made no cost-benefit analysis regarding the employment of a person with a disability, the director in case Netherlands 1 did indicate that the low level of investment required to make the workplace suitable was a significant factor: when, later in the person's period of employment, a special parking place

Summary of Barriers to Employment and Good Practice

Characteristic	Barriers to Employment	Good Practice
Workplace organisation and decision making	Need for flexible, multi-skilled self-directed employees, implies good work experience and higher educational level; Each new employee represents a significant increase in overall employment levels and associated costs; Individuals may be unable to assist a colleague with a disability	Faster and flatter decision making structures, with the possibility of a potential employee or mediating organisation meeting directly with the key decision maker
Recruitment practices	Unlikely to formulate clear or positive recruitment or equality of opportunity practices; Inappropriate use of questions about health or disability status on application forms	Telephone applications can lead to interviews without questioning of medical or health status; Faster and flatter decision making structures, with the possibility of a potential employee or mediating organisation meeting directly with the key decision maker
Attitudes towards disability	Prejudice about disability, especially related to a fear of unpredictability or the unknown; Concern about social image or awareness may reveal attitudes about disability that impose limits on areas of recruitment and progression	The use of personal experience to respond positively to an application or pro-actively seek out a person with a disability; Concern about social image or awareness can arise out of the desire to be a 'positive employer' and 'set a good example'
Enterprise trade sector	Health care enterprises and manufacturing services may be better disposed to the employment of people with disabilities	Enterprises in other trade sectors may be less familiar with people with disabilities and less disposed to their employment
Employment terms and conditions	Inappropriate use of opportunities to adopt lower terms and conditions of employment	Opportunities to try out work before entering into conventional or permanent employment contracts
Workplace Accessibility	Accessibility to premises provides a significant physical barrier to people with mobility or sensory disabilities	

was required, it was an advantage that it could be built by the employer's own staff at little cost.

In the Irish studies, all enterprises had physical access difficulties to a greater or lesser extent and none of the employers had any basic information about the assistance they could call on to adapt their buildings and facilities.

Easily identifiable access to financial support is important to overcome access barriers. Britain, where the new Disability Discrimination Act places an obligation on employers of 20 or more staff to make 'reasonable adjustments' to facilitate the employment of people with disabilities, the researchers speculated on the costs of removing physical barriers in many small enterprises. Indeed, the cost of such adaptations were, in one case discussed, expected by the employer to be beyond the capacity of public funding schemes. Improvements might also raise future rental costs and reduce affordability still further:

> "interest in the potential of Access to Work [a financial support programme] was sparked by the obstacles identified in employing a wheelchair user with highly desirable skills. In one case, assistance with internal physical alterations would sway the employment decision. In a second case, where readjustment of working routines would also be needed, costly and difficult major alterations were assumed to be beyond the scope of a government-funded programme and likely to impose costs on the employer..." (UK national report).

Additional environmental barriers, such as poor heating methods, which make premises cheap and affordable to small businesses, may compound health and safety risks in the workplace, and increase the vulnerability of people with disabilities to accident or illness.

Mediating Organisations

Mediating Organisations:

*   Matching candidates to needs;
*   Information provision;
*   Reducing risk;
*   On the job support;
*   Promoting confidence and self-esteem;
*   Differentiating between mediating organisations.

Introduction

The case studies presented are typically limited to companies who have employed people through the specialist mediating organisations: state or voluntary placement agencies and self help organisations. As a result, some of the conclusions reached about the overall picture of employees with disabilities in small businesses might be distorted. The absence in most national studies of evidence of alternative routes into employment would in many ways refute this possibility and, even so, the significance of mediating organisations appears to be dramatic.

- In France "Numerous informants told us that employers in general and owners of small businesses in particular do not want to spend their time studying the conditions under which disabled persons can be successfully integrated. That has to happen automatically, or else they will want someone to sort out the problems for them. That is why they are particularly interested in the type of "after-sales" service available to them from the teams that monitor the integration process." (French national report).

- In Ireland, "the agencies were a crucial factor in the employment of people with disabilities in our four companies. With the exception of Enterprise 2 – which is unusual in that a former employee in such an agency went out on his own and continued the work of the agency himself – all of the other employers recruited their employees with disabilities exclusively through agencies." (Irish national report)

- In the Netherlands, "In all three cases, help in making contact with potential employers played a part. In case 1, an employee prepared the way by talking to the director about the possibility of employing her friend, who was disabled. In cases 2 and 3 it was professional mediators who made the first contact with the employer." (Dutch national report)

- In the UK, "The involvement of an intermediary is important in bringing disabled people to the gates of employment, through assistance in job search and facilitated introductions." "Given the method used to recruit two of the employers interviewed, it was not surprising to find higher levels of awareness of, and satisfaction with, agencies acting as intermediaries to support the employment of disabled people." (UK national report)

Mediating organisations function by matching their clients to vacancies in enterprises. By adopting a proactive approach, making the initial contact with companies, employers are saved many of the time and financial costs of advertising and recruiting, and of securing any necessary aids and adaptations. By approaching the employer directly, the mediating body can ensure that there is less competition for their own clients.

- In Spain, the mediating organisation "designed a plan for the social integration and employment of young people with Down's Syndrome and, furthermore, set in train an effective procedure for liaison between companies in Barcelona and job seekers with that mental disability. They established a network of contacts, information and training with companies and, with job seekers, a system of personal development, vocational training and work monitoring in ordinary companies."

- In Germany "It is usually the officials from the employment office who bring up the possibility of additional assistance; only in a few cases do employers specifically enquire about it. The applications for assistance are usually completed or prepared as far as possible by the employment offices to prevent mistakes, particularly as there are a number of different forms involved. Most employers find the procedure straightforward, mainly because the officials responsible for placing disabled workers try to minimise the amount of effort involved." (German national report).

Matching Candidates to Needs

Achieving a good match between the ability of the person with a disability and the particular job was seen by employers in each Member State as being of crucial importance. The reliability of mediating agencies in achieving this was notable. The British research team found that:

"Agencies' familiarity with the local labour market and the needs of employers meant that they brought forward realistic candidates for the job. The specialist agencies in the study compared favourably with Job Centres operated by [state] Employment Services. The latter were thought often to send uncommitted applicants obliged to demonstrate their job-seeking performance in order to receive their Jobseeker's Allowance (unemployment benefit)." "Confidence in the agency meant that employers were prepared to consider their candidates if they had the right skills and aptitudes for work in the enterprise. Promotion of individuals with the right skills appears to be the key to the success of support agencies' intervention. (UK national report).

Similarly in the Netherlands:

"In the cases involving professional mediators, and probably also in the case where the friend/employee stepped in, there was some prior assessment of the potential, limitations and interests of the person with the disability. The mediators could make a professional assessment of the suitability of the job in view of the potential of the disabled candidates. In this way they were able to put forward one or more candidates who were likely to be suitable to the employers in cases 2 and 3." (Dutch national report).

Success in one instance promoted future interaction:

"most placements appear to result from a proactive agency bringing forward an acceptable person to fill the job. Having engaged an agency-supported employee, employers may be disposed to approach the agency themselves when further vacancies arise. In the case where the workforce was more stable and vacancies relatively rare, a support agency had less appeal to the employer." (UK national report).

Information Provision

Unlike most employers, mediating organisations are familiar with the subsidies and other forms of financial support available, and can facilitate the application process. In Britain, for example:

"The government's supported placement and DWA programmes are designed to supplement the wages of disabled people who are, respectively, less productive and limited by disability in the amount they earn. Support agencies play an important role in telling disabled people about the schemes, calculating the financial consequences and assisting with the application procedures." (UK national report).

Reducing Risk

The perceived risk to the employer of the 'unquantifiable' or unknown in employing a person with a disability was also targeted by mediating organisations. In Spain:

"In none of the three cases was there an official policy of promoting employment for people with disabilities, although in both case no. 1 and case no. 2, the enterprise did make an unwritten decision to hire people with disabilities until they reached the target of at least 2% of their staff. In both cases, they greatly appreciate the role played by the supported employment organizations, which helped them to carry out this policy with a maximum of guarantees from the point of view of the enterprise's interests." (Spanish national report)

The use of alternatives to the traditional employment contract were adopted in both Ireland and the Netherlands, with the aim of reducing the risk to an employer of employing someone whose ability is perceived to be in doubt. In Ireland:

> "candidates typically joined the company on work experience programmes, which meant that both employees and employer could use it as a trial to assess suitability without any commitment. The advantage of this approach, according to the NRB [state rehabilitation body], is that it circumvents the problems of the application process mentioned above, and gives a person a good chance of being retained. The advantage to the employer is that they are not taking too great a risk initially." (Irish national report).

In the Netherlands, the Industrial Insurance Board's executive office itself took on the role of employer, seconding its employees to an enterprise for a trial period. "The aim is to encourage the employer to take on the disabled worker by providing for a trial period entailing a low risk for the employer." (Dutch national report).

On-the-Job Support

Employee and employer needs may, in many cases, be long term in nature – focusing not solely on recruitment but also on integration and development. The recognition of this continuing involvement by mediating organisations relieves employers' concerns about possible demands on them if problems arise. In Ireland:

> "Employees are typically placed by the agencies under the Supported Employment Scheme which provides job coaches to train the person on site, personal development and ongoing support for both employee and employer. This support can greatly increase the employee's capacity to settle into the job, and it reassures employers that if problems arise in the future there will be support in dealing with it. Given that 'fear of the unknown' underlies the attitudes of many employers, this structured support would seem to be a crucial factor in their decision to take a chance." (Irish national report).

This commitment to the longer term also encourages the participation of people with disabilities who might otherwise be wary of testing their ability to work:

> "The prospects of retaining the job also affect access. Here, on-going support from the agency was, for some disabled people, an influential

factor. Where they were unsure about their ability to cope with the pressures of working, anticipated deterioration in their condition or foresaw problems with the working environment, knowledge that help was on hand, from someone who understood their situation, encouraged them to give work a try." (UK national report).

Promoting Employee Confidence and Self-Esteem

The employees with disabilities who participated in the case studies exhibited a strong motivation and preference for work. Employers are most keen on confident employees who have strong motivation and who focus on their ability more than what they are not able to do. At the same time, people with a disability are faced with a dilemma in overcoming the identified barriers, often resulting from negative perceptions of their ability.

Mediating organisations provide services and personal support to enable people with disabilities to manage these better, supplementing encouragement and support from family members and friends with training and one-to-one support at each of three phases: pre-application, during the recruitment process, and during employment:

"agencies were particularly helpful to disabled people who lacked confidence in their ability to manage at work or who were constrained in identifying and pursuing opportunities. The promise of support once in employment may encourage them to give work a try." (UK national report).

Differentiating Between Mediating Organisations

Mediating Organisations are not the only type of support available to a person with a disability. In some case studies, notably in the Netherlands, family and friends also acted as advocates or mediators. As in Spanish case study Spain 1, they each acted in collaboration with a specialist mediating organisation:

"Nonetheless, various other elements were involved in achieving success in this case: the person's *parents* and his *teachers* at the State school, who fostered favourable attitudes towards his social integration under normal conditions; *public funding*, in this case through the Generalitat of Catalonia and the European HORIZON programme, which enabled the employment-promotion activity of the Aura Project, a private organization, to be funded ...; the service enterprise which hired the person with a disability, at the level of both the personnel department and his own work colleagues and, in particular, his guardian, appointed by the enterprise to mediate between the worker suffering from Down's Syndrome and the other parties involved" (Spanish national report).

The nature and role of mediating organisations varied between Member States. While all received public funding (sometimes through short term programmes such as HORIZON, as in the above case), key differentials appear to be the legal status of the body: public or voluntary sector, and the scope of the organisation in relation to training and personal development.

In the majority of case studies (France, Germany, Netherlands, UK), the mediating organisations involved were statutory bodies. In the Irish and Spanish studies, voluntary agencies predominated. Despite these variations, there are few indications by which to judge the relative success of different types of mediating body. In particular, the low number of case studies and the employer focus of the research mean that little comparative material has been gathered on mediating organisations.

The German study looked at the role of the separate state welfare and placement agencies in some detail, concluding that:

*   the placement agencies are not integrated with each other or with training or welfare agencies and need to be approached by people with disabilities looking for work;

*   placement officers can focus on job seekers or employers, acting as a bridge between both. However, staff shortages mean that they are each responsible for an average of 650 unemployed people, plus companies, making regular contact with firms the exception rather than the rule. Placement officers are, "in many cases", "too busy" to realistically assess the potential employee's ability to do the job (German national report);

*   "work relating to the special protection against dismissal enjoyed by disabled workers takes up a considerable proportion of welfare officials' time": "at best they provided crisis management at the request of the disabled workers or the employers" (German national report);

*   the agencies were not very flexible or pro-active, for example: "Only a few of the officials saw it as part of their job to try to find new employment opportunities for the disabled in firms with which they already had contact" (German national report);

*   "Once a worker has been successfully placed the formal responsibility of the employment office is at an end, since any accompanying technical or financial assistance for firms is provided by central or local welfare offices"

(German national report). This means a change in support staff coupled with limitations arising out of separate data collection and storage systems used by each body for data protection purposes.

In terms of the scope of mediating organisations, most such agencies appear to integrate the role of training and development provider with that of finding placements. In Germany, again, where these functions are not integrated, there appears to be an identified need:

"From the very start of efforts to place disabled workers on the regular labour market there should be support measures which are not primarily job-related, but which also encourage the development of life skills in line with workers' job prospects. If they do not have any definite ideas about their future career, employment and welfare offices should offer them vocational and personal guidance and advice." (German national report)

Despite the limitations apparent in this German approach to placement and mediation, there is insufficient case study material or comparative information in other Member States to distinguish effectively between types of organisation and scope of service provision.

Summary of Barriers to Employment and Good Practice

Characteristic	Barriers to Employment	Good Practice
Matching candidates to needs		Identifying the needs of employers and matching these with candidates for employment
Information provision		Providing information on personal, financial and technical support available
Reducing risk		Providing supported employment strategies
On the job support		Provide continued support for the employee and employer
Promoting confidence and self-esteem		Promoting confidence and self-esteem through personal support and training for people with disabilities
Differentiating between mediating organisations	Some public sector agencies perhaps less likely to offer detailed needs identification and integrated, continued support?	

Chapter 6

Conclusions and Policy Implications

Introduction

This study is a qualitative analysis of the situation in six EU Member States, based upon a small series of case studies and verification action in each country. As such, it has a primary emphasis on the practical experiences of people with disabilities employed in small and medium sized enterprises. It focuses on successful examples of the integration of disabled people in employment to enable the identification of good practice as well as barriers.

The sample size is necessarily small and, as such, it has limitations: the small number of cases studied, the unrepresentative sample, the situations that could not be examined. It is not known, for example, if the profile of mediating organisation clients differ from the profile of all people with disabilities who are of working age, in particular regarding the nature of their disabilities and level of educational attainment. However, in this and other recent studies of people with disabilities in the workplace, only very limited numbers of such people are in employment in small or medium sized enterprises. There are very few role models.

Nevertheless, the study outcomes allow a clear development in our understanding of the way employers make decisions, the reasons behind their decisions and their impact. There would appear to be a high degree of commonality in the actual experiences and situations in each of the Member States studied, regardless of definitions of disability or preferences for voluntary or mandatory action. In itself this would suggest the veracity of the study findings.

There is no blueprint for an effective legislative and regulatory framework:

- Financial incentives have a key facilitative role but, as they currently operate, do not necessarily meet the needs of either employers or employees, and do not reflect technological or labour market trends;

- Despite differences in the applicability and enforcement of employment quotas and anti-discrimination legislation, these appear to have little practical effect on SME employer behaviour;

- Health and safety and insurance regulations are perceived by employers as an impediment to the employment of people with disabilities;

- Educational attainment is low among people with disabilities;

- Women, older people with disabilities and those with more severe disabilities appear to face additional barriers in accessing employment;

- Recruitment practices rarely recognise the value of equal opportunity and other good recruitment practices;

- Low confidence and self-esteem among employees, and attitudes of both work colleagues and employers can limit the degree to which an employee successfully integrates and progresses within a firm;

- The attitudes of employers of people with a disability demonstrate the striking importance of personal experience of disability;

- Mediating organisations play a pivotal role in promoting a positive awareness both of disability and of the regulatory framework, providing training and personal support to people with disabilities and their employers.

This chapter seeks to provide some conclusions on these issues. As small and medium sized enterprises do not exist in isolation, the nature of the concerns and issues raised are such that many of the policy recommendations made are more broadly applicable.

Financial Incentives for Employees

To promote the take-up of employment opportunities, it is essential to separate out financial support related to a disability from financial support due to economic inactivity. The costs attached to managing a disability do not diminish as income increases. These are primarily associated with travel to and from work, the physical accessibility of work, living and social facilities, personal care needs and interpretative needs. While a case can easily be made for maintaining means testing, the likelihood of a flat-rate entitlement system being abused is low once a clear case for an individual's need has been established.

For many people with disabilities, part-time work or work with flexible hours is seen as particularly desirable. The high value attached to such opportunities might also apply to many people with a chronic or cyclical illness, enabling work during periods of health and the take up of health care when unwell. Part time and other introductory forms of work allow people to determine the likelihood with which they could explore full-time, long-term employment opportunities. Teleworking and other forms of flexible and home-based employment can offer long term employment solutions that might not adequately be recognised or facilitated in terms of state financial support. Legislation and policy on financial support for people with disabilities currently lags behind legislation and policies on the Information Society and trends in labour market flexibility.

In some Member states, notably Britain and Ireland, part-time or flexible work is permitted without a negative impact on personal or family income only within clearly defined limits. In some cases, only if work is perceived to be of therapeutic benefit and prior authorisation is given; in other cases only up to a low earnings or hours threshold. The problems with these approaches lie in: their narrowness; the low time or income threshold before family income becomes affected; the short life of therapeutic earnings schemes (how long is work 'therapeutic' for, and when has it achieved this purpose?); and the perception of people with disabilities and employers that schemes are exceptional, punitive rather than facilitative, with the object of recouping state funds at the earliest opportunity. Most people with disabilities, given historic limitations to their access to higher education and training, will currently be entering the job market for low paid, less skilled work. The impact of these factors is therefore all the greater.

Consideration should be given to the evaluation of the effectiveness of income support measures and the introduction of greater flexibility to reflect a greater diversity in employment and work situations such as earnings disregards.

Financial Incentives for Employers

A wide range of subsidies and incentives to employers are available from state bodies in each Member State, with a remit focusing on workplace adaptations, interpretative and personal care needs. Some types of incentive are more successful than others. Flat rate premiums are believed by many to devalue employees, while wage subsidies need to take into account the full cost of any underperformance or increased supervision.

Take up, particularly among small and medium sized enterprises is minimal. Employers - particularly in countries without an implemented employment quota - are largely unaware of the existence of such schemes and people with disabilities appear unsure about how such schemes can be of personal benefit.

The collection of a number of previous British aids and adaptations programmes under a single banner ('Access to Work') is helpful in that it makes the support available more legible to employers and potential employees. However, the profile and implementation mechanisms for this and other schemes appears to be low as a consequence of poor transmission of information to employers. Greater awareness is likely, of course, to lead to greater demand for resources.

In some cases, negative assumptions have been made by employers about their applicability, value and lengthy, bureaucratic approach. In other cases, such assumptions have been confirmed. In two of the cases studied, the continued employment of people with disabilities was put at risk.

Consideration should be given to the formal evaluation of such programmes, including reasons for approvals and refusals, drop out rates and financial limits. Programmes should be flexibly designed to promote employment protection and progression as well as new employment opportunities, to reflect the progressive, cyclical or fluctuating nature of many disabilities as well as those which might arise during the course of employment.

Compulsory Employment Obligations

Employment Quotas are applied in three of the six studied Member States. No quota scheme in any of the Member States studied has achieved its target and in some, like Germany, performance has worsened. Quota schemes are controversial measures to some. Employers, unsurprisingly, prefer voluntary action and incentives while organisations representing the interests of people with disabilities would favour more strict enforcement and strengthen penalties for non-compliance to improve performance.

The contribution of this study to the debate on the value of quota schemes is limited. Many small companies are not the targets of quota legislation. Of the nine cases in the three countries with implemented quota schemes, only four were subject to quota requirements; five, by virtue of their small size, were exempt.

In no case in this study was filling a quota the sole or primary objective, selecting a candidate capable of undertaking the vacant job was invariably the business priority. The consequences for non-compliance among those that are subject to the quota were perceived to be minor.

Employer behaviour and attitudes among SMEs studied would appear to be similar in Member States both with and without employment quotas. However, quotas do seem, on occasion to add weight to the argument that a person with a disability should be employed rather than an alternative candidate, either as a form of moral persuasion or as an unwritten practical justification. The value of broader, anti-discrimination policies over compartmentalised policies such as quota schemes is untested.

Health and Safety and Insurance Regulations

In several Member States, employers perceive that the costs associated with complying with legal requirements for Public Liability and Employers' Liability Insurance will be burdensome. A clear and unnecessary negative link that can impede access to employment for people with disabilities has been made between health and safety at work and disability by many employers.

This partly appears to be an information gap, and its rectification could form part of awareness raising programmes. Partly, however, it is related to actual insurance costs incurred by companies who employ or service people with disabilities. While it is less common for such costs to increase for Employers' and Public Liability, it is applied as a general rule to sickness and health-related insurances. The case study evidence – and additional quantitative research conducted in the Netherlands – suggests that there is a conflict between actuarial decisions and employment promotion measures funded by Member States.

Demographic trends towards more ageing populations more prone to develop disabilities, together with advances in genetic testing suggest that this problem will grow in significance. Given the key importance of employment promotion, the provision of insurance cover to individuals and organisations should not exclude people who are potentially economically active. The use of alternative insurance risk rating methods, such as the 'community rating' principle that applies to the Irish health insurance sector, could be explored.

In some countries, notably the Netherlands, the sheer complexity of the sickness insurance system and resultant re-integration measures raises significant concerns about the cost of compliance and implementation for small and medium sized companies. Particularly for smaller enterprises, developing a full awareness of the current system and forthcoming changes is a formidable task.

The European Commission has acknowledged, in the 1994 White Paper on Growth, Competitiveness and Employment that "complex legal and administrative burdens arising from employment protection legislation represent a drain on the employment capacity of all enterprises, that they reduce the operating efficiency and increase costs, and that they have a relatively greater impact on SMEs." Clarity and simplicity are essential to enable small employers to maintain their viability and adhere to good employment and other practices.

Education and Training for People with Disabilities

Education and training provision is fundamental to the development of employment aspirations, work-related skills and the ability to grasp opportunities. In most Member States studied, the availability of educational opportunities and training services to the same standard as that enjoyed by the 'mainstream' appeared to be lacking.

Without adequate or comparable education and training, people with disabilities are likely to find only low skill, low wage (and high supply) work open to them. This is particularly onerous given the likelihood of relatively higher transportation, medical or other costs incurred in managing a disability.

A long-term approach to prevent the formation of negative attitudes generally is to have more emphasis on integrated schooling, instead of special school systems for people with disabilities. Not only might this ensure the delivery of same standard schooling, integration through the promotion of personal contact between those with and without disabilities is essential to change attitudes, as can be evidenced by the number of employers studied for whom prior experience of disability was critical. Many organisations involved in promoting the rights of people with disabilities favour the provision of disability awareness training and use of trainers who themselves experience a disability for this reason.

Mediating organisations that place people with disabilities in employment are also, in many Member States, the agencies that offer post-school vocational training. This continuity - and narrow target group focus - enables them to provide integrated specialist services, and build up a relationship that can promote self-esteem, and define employment objectives and career options.

Such an approach clearly supports people who are not able to undertake mainstream training opportunities but might not meet the needs of people who do not (or who do not wish to) self-identify as having a disability. These specialist skills, knowledge and experience need to be supplemented by training and supported employment opportunities offered jointly by mainstream and specialist providers.

Recruitment Practices

There was little evidence in the case studies of discrimination against people with disabilities, unsurprisingly given the study focus on examples of successful recruitment and retention. Recruitment practices had both positive and negative characteristics. Positive characteristics lay in the directness, flexibility and informality of recruitment processes in small and medium sized enterprises. Negative tendencies arose through inflexibility in job specifications and working practices and a lack of awareness of good recruitment practices. Typical recruitment methods included personal recommendations or a 'first come, first served' approach that did not recognise the value of equal opportunity practices. The added dimensions of age and gender are also a cause for concern.

Much of this is related to a lack of information on alternatives to current practices, including the promotion of good recruitment practices and the promotion of people with disabilities as capable of employment.

Attitudes towards Disability

Employers, employees and mediating organisations across the Member States studied have remarked on negative attitudes towards disability and a general lack of awareness of issues associated with disability and work. A person with a disability is rarely seen as the best candidate for a job because employers fear that the candidate might be of limited ability, have an unpredictable or high rate of sickness, or are simply an unnecessary additional risk. In taking these attitudes, employers are strongly influenced by negative views of disability: in reality a disability is not necessarily coupled with higher absenteeism, lower productivity or risk.

The case studies demonstrate the striking importance of a positive personal or social attitude by employers. The key issue lies in raising the awareness of employers to both the benefits of employing people with disabilities and of programmes of support that can facilitate this, including the promotion of positive non-charitable attitudes towards people with disabilities that can tackle the critical issue of ability rather than liability.

Mediating Organisations

Given the absence of identifiable alternative integration models, the role of the mediating organisation is clearly a pivotal one for many people with a disability in terms of recruitment, integration, training and development.

Employers have emphasised the importance of matching the job to an appropriate individual and the value of cost and time savings. Employees have acknowledged the importance of specialist assistance to overcome awareness and discrimination barriers, and to understand their own individual needs. Both recognise the importance of continuing support on-the-job.

Information provision regarding financial incentives or required workplace adaptations has, in many cases studied, been incomplete without the provision of assistance in accessing those schemes. Mediating agencies generally appear familiar with financial support measures available, and can take care of the applications and arrangements on behalf of an employer. The use of both temporary contracts and secondments with a state body or mediating organisation functioning as the legal employer can be beneficial when possible at no risk to either employee or employer.

Chapter 7   Recommendations

Introduction

There are three key areas of common concern across Member States:

- the need for the development of a greater awareness and understanding of disability among employers;

- a need for better dissemination of information for employers on the regulatory framework and how it supports and facilitates the employment of people with disabilities;

- the indispensable nature of mediating organisations.

These commonalities are interdependent. On the one hand, the provision of information about the regulatory framework is incomplete without practical support and assistance to access available programmes. On the other hand, mediating organisations are hampered in their effectiveness by a lack of awareness by employers of the abilities and aspirations of people with disabilities.

Awareness

The need for positive and tightly-focused educational and awareness raising measures applicable to small and medium sized enterprises is one of the clearest outcomes of this study. The key role of personal experience as a motivational factor for employers has been highlighted, as has the prevalence of perceptions of disability based on fears of risk, incapacity (rather than ability) and absenteeism. These demonstrate both the possibilities created by good practice and familiarity with people with disabilities, and the need for broad and positive, awareness raising initiatives. Employer perceptions should be challenged in three areas:

Challenging Perceptions		
Absenteeism	**Capacity and ability**	**Risk**
using evidence to challenge perceptions of sickness and absenteeism among people with disabilities	demonstrating the abilities of people with disabilities	stressing ways in which the risks of employing people can be reduced through the use of mediating organisations

Such initiatives should focus on positive examples and case studies appropriate to small and medium sized enterprises. The relevance of new information and communication technologies and working methods should also be explored.

Information

Many of the study conclusions focus on concern about information provision. The inadequacy of information dissemination methods has arisen in relation to employment protection measures, the availability of financial incentives (including the procedures by which they are accessed) and in the promotion of good recruitment and employment practices.

Information Dissemination		
Financial Incentives	**Recruitment Practices**	**Information Related to Specific Disabilities**
the provision of information on the availability of financial incentives and the means by which they are accessed	the provision of information on good recruitment and employment practices and procedures	practical information, where necessary, to enable the making of informed judgements and decisions about a candidate's suitability

Information needs can be identified not only at the recruitment level, but also in subsequent induction and developmental stages. While there is a overlap with broad awareness raising initiatives — particularly in the context of promoting good practice through awareness of the value of good recruitment and employment practices — there is a clear role in information provision and dissemination for mediating organisations.

Mediating Organisations

The use of specialist mediating organisations appears to significantly improve the chances of employment for people with disabilities. Mediating organisations function by matching their clients to vacancies in enterprises. By adopting a proactive approach, making the initial contact with companies, the level of perceived risk to employers is reduced. Employers are saved many of the time and financial costs of advertising and recruiting, and of securing any necessary aids and adaptations. By approaching the employer directly, the mediating body can ensure that there is less competition for their own clients. They also assist clients to overcome barriers arising out of low educational attainment, poor confidence and low self esteem. Despite this, several factors remain untested or unexamined and should form the subject of further study:

- defining operational principles;

- are specialist mediating agencies preferable to integrated mainstream provision?

- what are the most effective methodologies and models used by mediating organisations, could the concept of 'route counselling' or 'pathways to integration' help to deepen existing approaches?

- defining roles and responsibilities regarding information provision, advice, counselling, training and, potentially, employment.

References

European Commission (1994) White Paper on Growth, Competitiveness and Employment, Brussels.

European Foundation for the Improvement of Living and Working Conditions (1997) Case Studies on Employment of People with Disabilities in Small and Medium Sized Enterprises, France, Working Paper No. WP/97/57/EN, Dublin.

European Foundation for the Improvement of Living and Working Conditions (1997) Case Studies on Employment of People with Disabilities in Small and Medium Sized Enterprises, Germany, Working Paper No. WP/97/60/EN, Dublin.

European Foundation for the Improvement of Living and Working Conditions (1997) Case Studies on Employment of People with Disabilities in Small and Medium Sized Enterprises, Ireland, Working Paper No. WP/97/58/EN, Dublin.

European Foundation for the Improvement of Living and Working Conditions (1997) Case Studies on Employment of People with Disabilities in Small and Medium Sized Enterprises, Netherlands, Working Paper No. WP/97/61/EN, Dublin.

European Foundation for the Improvement of Living and Working Conditions (1997) Case Studies on Employment of People with Disabilities in Small and Medium Sized Enterprises, Spain, Working Paper No. WP/97/59/EN, Dublin.

European Foundation for the Improvement of Living and Working Conditions (1997) Case Studies on Employment of People with Disabilities in Small and Medium Sized Enterprises, United Kingdom, Working Paper No. WP/97/83/EN, Dublin.

Eurostat (1995) Disabled Persons, Statistical Data, Second Edition, Brussels.

Lunt, N, and Thornton, P (1993) Employment Policies for Disabled People, A review of legislation and services in fifteen countries. Research Series No. 16. Employment Department, London.

Moreno, E, and Valera, S (1992) Actitud de l'Empresa Privada davant la integració laboral de persones amb disminció (Attitude of Private Enterprise towards the Employment of People with Disabilities), Municipal Institute for the Disabled, Barcelona.

Richter and Stackelbeck (1995) Aktion-Integration Program, Dortmund.

Thornton P and Lunt N (1997) Employment Policies for Disabled People in Eighteen Countries: A Review. Social Policy Research Unit, University of York.

Glossary

AGEFIPH, Association nationale de Gestion du Fonds pour l'insertion professionnelle des handicapés (National Association for the Administration of the Fund for the Professional Integration of People with Disabilities), (France) is a non-profit making organisation managed by representatives of social partners. It collects voluntary contributions payable by enterprises which do not meet employment quota targets and finances campaigns to promote the employment of people with disabilities, as well as supporting access to jobs, redeployment and professional development. Despite lacking obligations under the quota, small businesses are eligible for AGEFIPH funds.

Asociación Las Encinas (Spain), a local non-profit making education and training body formed by people with disabilities and their families and professionals in Guadalajara region. The Association manages a vocational training centre and a Special Employment Centre supported by the Horizon programme.

Aura (Spain) is one of a number of small local training and placement bodies. Aura is a nonprofit-making body established in Barcelona in 1989 to support young people with Down's Syndrome who are registered and who wish to work and become independent. It is financially supported by the government of Catalonia (Labour Department of the Generalitat) and, since 1992, the Horizon programme.

Bedrijfsverenigingen, Industrial Insurance Boards or Associations (Netherlands). These statutory social insurance bodies were until 1 January 1997 responsible for social insurance benefits and provisions for employees (unemployment, sickness and disability). Within this framework they assessed personal and workplace aids and adaptations. Since 1 January 1997 the

Bedrijfsverenigingen have been replaced by the National Institution for Social Insurances (LISV) which contracts out the administration of employees' insurance schemes to five private social security agencies. **GAK** is by far the largest of these. Activities concerning mediation for people with disabilities are to be transferred to the labour market services.

COTOREP, Commissions techniques d'orientation et de reclassement professionel (Technical Commission for the Registration and Assessment of Disability), (France) is a commission responsible for registration and assessment in each département. It is responsible for granting assistance in the form of allowances and guidance to adults with disabilities and accords official recognition as "disabled workers", on which entitlement to most employment-promotion benefits depends.

CRPs, occupational retraining centres, (France) are specialised vocational training centres for people with disabilities. In order to receive training at a CRP, an applicant must normally have been recognised as having a disability by a **COTOREP** or have been the victim of an occupational accident. These are not the only training centres that are accessible to people with disabilities but play a dominant role.

EAL, 'Employment Consultancy and Integration Team' (Spain), of the Barcelona Municipal Institute for the Disabled. This is an autonomous body within the City Council, which aims to promote access to the ordinary labour market - private and public-sector companies and government - for local people with a disability. Set up in 1985, the EAL was the first such service. It has received funding under several EU programmes.

Émergence (France) is a mediating organisation in the Ile-de-France region responsible for drawing up skill profiles, providing guidance and training, and approaching companies on behalf of people recognised by **COTOREP** as having a disability. Émergence also provides technical assistance to enterprises.

EPSRs, redeployment preparation and monitoring teams, (France) are responsible for preparing, administering and monitoring the entry of people with disabilities into employment. There is now an EPSR in each département, where they are one of the key mechanisms for the employment of people with disabilities. Entitlement to assistance from the EPSRs is generally dependent on prior recognition as a disabled worker by a **COTOREP.**

The European Foundation for the Improvement of Living and Working Conditions is an autonomous body of the European Community based in

Dublin, Ireland, that has as its main mission to produce, discuss and disseminate information and research to advise the European policymakers and social partners in order to contribute to the planning and establishment of better living and working conditions.

FÁS, Foras Áiseanna Saothair (Ireland), is the statutory agency responsible for training and placement of unemployed people. While not providing services specifically designed for people with disabilities, it gives priority for people registered with the **NRB** to a range of support schemes and initiatives including lump-sum premiums to employers, weekly subsidies and community employment.

Fürsorgestellen, local welfare offices (Germany), give personal assistance to people with disabilities in obtaining and retaining appropriate living accommodation and in travelling to and from the place of work. They promote participation in vocational training and co-operate with employee representatives. Specialist support according to the special kind of disability is also provided. The welfare offices often do not work in collaboration with employment services or rehabilitation related organisations, which were created and administered by separate legislation. Official recognition of a person's disability, required to secure access to support and services, has to be conducted separately by both institutions.

Gabinete Profesionales y Proyectos, 'Pro & Pro' (Spain). Professionals and Projects Consultancy is a private agency which has a commercial contract with the **Asociación Las Encinas** to promote the social integration and integration into employment of people trained at the Association's Special Employment Centre. Pro & Pro secure job placements, profile candidates, provide job preparation training and access support measures.

GAK-Detapool (Netherlands) was (it has since been renamed) a mediation unit of the Gemeenschappelijke Administratie Kantoor (GAK), the Joint Administration Office doing executive work for a number of **Bedrijfsverenigingen.** It provided work assessment and placement services for people with disabilities, including the employment and secondment of candidates.

Hauptfürsorgestellen, the 'Higher Public Assistance Agency' or central welfare office (Germany), monitors and enforces the legal rights and duties of both employers and people with disabilities. A Hauptfürsorgestelle has to give prior agreement if an employer wants to give notice to a person with a disability. It is funded by employers' quota compensation payments which are used to provide financial support for both employees and employers. Financial support for employers can be either permanent or for an initial period. Permanent support includes grants to the wages of people with disabilities. Initial financial support programmes are geared to the creation of new jobs and to promote the use of training and professional consultation by technical advice centres. It also provides training courses and conducts public relations work and research programmes.

Headway, an Irish **voluntary agency** focusing on support for people with head injuries.

The **HELIOS** programme — now completed — was set up by a European Council decision in 1993 with the aim of promoting equal opportunities and integration for people with disabilities. The programme had three key objectives; to develop and improve exchange and information activities with Member States and non-governmental organisations; to promote effective approaches and measures in order to achieve increased effectiveness and better co-ordination of actions; and to promote the development of a policy at community level of co-operation with Member States and the organisations and associations concerned with integration, based on the best innovative and effective experience and practice in Member States.

JobAhead (United Kingdom) is a local authority funded service, funded in similar ways to **JobReach.** It focuses on two main client groups: people with physical disabilities, and people with learning disabilities. JobAhead run direct training courses for disabled people who wanted to work, for example in basic skills, social skills, interview skills, and computer and keyboard techniques.

JobReach (United Kingdom) is a local authority service established in 1986 with additional funding from the European Social Fund, Training and Enterprise Councils and other national funding schemes. The overall aim of the agency is to support and help people with disabilities - particularly people with mental health difficulties - who wish to work, through assessment, 'pre-entry' services, such as a work placement or supervised voluntary work, and job introductions and ongoing support, including benefit advice and support to access financial support or equipment.

KARE, an Irish mediating agency related to the statutory Midland Health Board, Tullamore, Ireland.

NRB, National Rehabilitation Board (Ireland), this body co-ordinates and funds the work of disability organisations nationally, including the placement of people with disabilities in employment. The NRB is the main link between all disability-related services and organisations. It assesses people as having a disability for purposes of establishing eligibility for a means-tested Disability Allowance and for receiving priority places on **FÁS** training courses. The NRB is seen by other statutory bodies as having responsibility for everything relating to disability.

NTDI, National Training and Development Institute, formerly known as Rehab. An Irish **voluntary agency.**

Placement, Assessment and Counselling Teams, PACTs (United Kingdom), are local offices that are part of the Employment Services agency of the Department for Education and Employment (DfEE). These offer (or co-ordinate) employment preparation and placement services. Local offices have increasingly contracted out services to independent specialist agencies. The Department also operates the 'Access to Work' (ATW) programme of financial assistance and workplace aids and adaptations.

SMEs 'Small and Medium Sized Enterprises', defined variously to employ up to 250 or 500 people. The definition used in this study was under 500 employees.

STEP Enterprises, an Irish **voluntary agency**, responsible for placing people with disabilities in employment on behalf of St. John of God's.

Supported Employment agencies (United Kingdom) which place people with severe disabilities with host employers, offer support on the job and, under the national Supported Placements scheme, arrange supplements to the wages of those with reduced productivity.

Worklink, an Irish **voluntary agency**, the training and placement agency of Schizophrenia Ireland.

Voluntary Agencies (Ireland) The **NRB** contract out to voluntary agencies nationwide who provide specialist training and job placement services. These include **Worklink, Headway, STEP Enterprises** and the National Training and Development Institute **(NTDI).** Employment support measures include subsidies based on reduced productivity, part time job incentives and workplace adaptation grants.

European Foundation for the Improvement of Living and Working Conditions

The Employment of People with Disabilities in Small and Medium-sized Enterprises

Luxembourg: Office for Official Publications of the European Communities

1998 – 152 pp. – 16 cm x 23.5 cm

ISBN 92-828-2949-9

Price (excluding VAT) in Luxembourg: ECU 16